THE
POWER OF
YES!
IN INNOVATION

SHAWN R. NASON
With Contributions by Stephan D. Junion, PhD

Dedication

From Author Shawn R. Nason

To my wife, Carla, and two children Kayla and Kolby for your unconditional love and support as I follow my dreams, my wishes, and my passion. You have sacrificed so many things, and many times, me, so I can travel the country and world to help people find who they want to be when they grow up. Thank you for pushing me to be the best man, husband, father, and friend to all those around! Love you guys!

From Contributor Stephan D. Junion, PhD

To my wife, Cheryl, and three wonderful children, Seth, Madison, and Drew for your unwavering support and tolerance throughout all of my endeavors. Your love and support enable me to explore a world and subject that I am so passionate about. Thank you for helping me be the best I can be as a husband, father, and professional, in that order.

Acknowledgments

I would like to thank several people who have helped make this book come to life. First, to Stephan Junion: Not only did you contribute to this book, but you pushed me when I needed to be pushed. You challenged me when I needed to be challenged. But most importantly, you have been right by my side through this whole process. Best of luck on your next journey!

I would like to thank the editorial board for your input: Dr. Deborah Clary, Erik Eaker, Dr. James Oakley, and Simeon Sessley. Each of you brought a different perspective and voice. All of you are valued people in my life, and I hope you will be there as more books come to life.

I would like to thank Sean Slovenski. Over the years, you have believed in me, saw things in me, and given me opportunities that I would have never had. Many of those experiences are why this book is so important. Thank you!

Last but not least, I want to thank Cathy Fyock for coaching me along this journey and for putting great people in my path, like my publisher, Kate Colbert. Kate: There are not enough words to say how thankful Steve and I are to you helping us on this journey. I look forward to many more.

Table of Contents

SECTION 3

The Power of YES! in Innovation ...
Know Me, Surprise Me, Make it Easy   101

Prequel to *The Power of YES!* *in Innovation*: A History Lesson

Most books are a labor of love by one person. In this case, labor has been very long and Shawn and I are giving birth to this book jointly. This is Steve writing this portion because you'll find out later that Shawn has been a prolific blogger and we have stolen much of his content and refined it for this particular effort. It's impossible and somewhat unreasonable for us to write in a single voice as you continue to read, but we will do our best to limit the confusion. Each of our voices is here for a specific reason, as you will also see in the upcoming pages.

Also, you should know, unless otherwise stated, we have created everything you will read in this book. We may have offered insight as a leader or as an individual contributor to provide strategic value and perspective to benefit various scenarios you may encounter.

You will find that I have a different perspective of Shawn's work as we were business partners for a number of years immediately preceding the publication of this book. I don't always agree with Shawn, but I/ we do commit to the main emphasis of what each other has to say and we implicitly trust that the intention behind the statement is only in the other's best interests. This has taken time on both of our parts and we have had heated discussions at times. And, it has all been worth it. For example, sometimes we argue even though we agree on the same basic point! It might be the words we use or the half-shared sentences because we know each other so well, but our business and personal relationship works well. Our voices are unique and we both are passionate about bringing the consumer into clearer focus in this very opaque world.

I also told Shawn that it is important I write this introduction. Some may say Shawn is an over-the-top promoter of himself. I call bull-shit on that notion ... and yes, I swear and I've been trying to quit forever. I have at least committed to zero f-words, although there is a moderate level of cursing in this book because that's just how I am. In any case, Shawn really does downplay what he's accomplished. I was his business partner for a number of years and the crap that he has had to deal with — both within organizations and outside of organizations — has been tremendous. He has done some wicked cool work helping associates, colleagues, executives, etc., to under-stand the consumer. Shawn truly is an Executive of Getting Shit Done! So, I'll provide my perspective on how the genesis for this book came about. Shawn probably won't agree 100 percent, but he also won't over-edit because he trusts me.

Where to Begin?

It's hard to know where to start when describing the collective journey Shawn and I have been on. We could start with Shawn having more degrees than he needs or we could start with his work at Disney in finance where he eventually became a Walt Disney Imagineer. This is actually a fair point, so let me summarize a major life shift I have heard him speak of frequently. After being in finance and working with the Walt Disney Company, he got sick of telling people "No" to their requests as a finance guru. He wanted to open up to saying "Yes!" versus always being the "No" guy. This drove him from finance to consumer experience and innovation. To me, it still doesn't make sense — the finance element, not the rest.

Every time I look at Shawn, I think, *Finance? Really?* But yeah, he's really good with numbers that have a lot of digits. As an Imagineer, he realized there was a world of opportunities and instead of saying "No," he was able to say, "How might we ... " as it relates to the Disney experience, which still remains one of the best in the world for consumers. While Shawn's transformation has been the foundation for his mindset since those early days, it is also the mindset for this book — saying *YES! to the power of innovation* helped him become a new version of himself, one that is all about advocating for the consumer.

I think we need to fast forward a bit from Disney, and move into where he was hired away to — healthcare. I know, you are saying "What the hell?" Who would want to go into healthcare? Shawn did. It was both a personal and professional decision for him to take the leap of faith and move his family to Dallas. Shawn was in information technology for the shortest amount of time ever recorded (but he made the greatest connection in that time, both personally and professionally) – thank goodness for that, and let's talk about when we were both at one of the four major health insurers.

The Mississippi Delta

Shawn had just spent the better part of a year in Mississippi, driving many miles while working with a team to help establish health-care exchanges and improve health outcomes in approximately 50 counties. No one else wanted to set up shop in Mississippi because they didn't want to take on the unknowns of one of the most health-challenged areas and states in the country. The organization bet that we had the talent to do something special at that time and agreed to move forward with setting up the exchange. The challenge was that we knew very little about this part of the country. We learned quickly.

The truth about it is this: if you travel between Louisiana and Mississippi, in many categories, one state has a lower score than another in any one of a hundred health categories. Both states are unfortunately at or near the bottom in far too many of these important health and well-being categories. From a somewhat humorous perspective, it allows folks in Louisiana to say, "At least we aren't Mississippi" in X category while Mississippi says the same about Louisiana in categories where *they* are dead last.

You have to spend a lot of time in either state to appreciate and understand the depth of health disparity in this part of the country. And it's not about people being lazy and not wanting to take care of themselves. If that's what you think as you began reading this book, you need to get yourself right, as Dr. Phil might say, and throw out your preconceived notions about the good folks of Mississippi and Louisiana. As a matter of fact, whatever preconceived notions you have about people (we overuse the term consumer too much I think, even in this book), you need to start with empathy and understanding as we have learned so many times.

Mississippi became a true spark in the organization and in the world of consumerism. Shawn was an early leader, pioneer and champion of the consumer within the organization and was assigned, along with a team, to "figure out" Mississippi. Having been a Disney Imagineer, he was well-steeped in the world of the consumer. He even looked the part. As one of the senior executives told him in a meeting during his work in Mississippi regarding his Converse sneakers, and less-than-conforming "smart casual" office attire, "Don't change the way you dress ... we need to [shake] things up ... "

Shawn was definitely a mover and shaker and it showed up in Mississippi. He was leading and part of a small team that really was the genesis of consumer innovation for the organization, focused on proving out a methodology and process that yielded at least one patent application and a tremendous amount of knowledge about the people of Mississippi.

Shifting to San Antonio

Fast forward. As Mississippi began to wind down, I would frequently see Shawn storming up and down the aisle where I resided. Shawn wasn't coming to see me, though, he was working with one of our colleagues, another amazing consumer experience expert. One day, Shawn decided to stop by my cube and we began some small talk regarding my Ph.D. dissertation – I had big cardboard diagrams left over in my cube from conferences where I had just presented my work. Shawn was working on his DBA (Doctorate in Business Administration) as well at that time. As we spoke, we learned each of us was focused on a qualitative approach to understanding our topic through interviews – making meaning through the words and wisdom of other people. Instantly, I realized we were kindred spirits. This led Shawn to nominate me and pull me in to get my Innovation Engineering Black Belt. While I have many thoughts about this experience, the result was fantastic. I learned how to translate decades of focusing on the learner into focusing on the consumer with about 100 new tools in my toolkit!

At about the same time that Shawn was helping to lead the innovation revolution, the company was beginning to expand beyond the great work by the team in Mississippi and the next stop selected was

San Antonio. Many lessons were learned in Mississippi; however, there was still no playbook. In addition, our CEO needed to get a larger group of executives on board if this approach was going to go viral within the organization. Shawn and I were in the midst of negotiating a full day session with the CEO, his direct reports, and the top 108 executives regarding our strategy in San Antonio. Even though the title of this book is *The Power of YES! In Innovation*, we had to say no about a million times to our CEO and to the sponsors of this effort. Some of my favorite "Nos" include:

1. No, we are not going to cut this down to a 2-hour session!

2. Yes, we need the full day! Stop asking! Please!

3. No, we are NOT going to publish an agenda no matter how many times you ask or if you ask me or Shawn separately.

4. Trust us, you've invested thousands of development dollars in us to gain new skills and test out the methodology. We've got this!

Eventually, they relented, mostly willingly, to our version of YES! We finalized intense planning for both an immersion experience the evening prior as well as a full-day strategy session.

Our relationship went to a whole new level the night before we brought over 100 executives into an ideation session. We had been working on designing an immersion experience the night before with our colleagues so they could better understand and put themselves into the shoes of our consumers before the strategy session. We wanted our executives to experience what our Hispanic colleagues and community members experienced as part of the community.

Furniture Matters

In all his infinite wisdom, Shawn knew we had to create an environment where executives could fully engage in the strategy session we had designed. If you have ever sat on a standard hotel chair for more than an hour, your ass will tell you it's not very comfortable. So, Shawn did what Shawn does. He rented 70's style pleather (fake leather) furniture from around the region. We actually took all of the furniture we could find in Louisville, Indiana, and Cincinnati and brought it to the hotel. The trucks began rolling in about 11:00 p.m. The team that delivered didn't have a full crew and we were getting nervous because we had to get the physical space right to encourage the right mindset going into the next day's session. How wrong were we!

Shawn is a light sleeper and my cell phone rang about 3:00 a.m. to say the entire room was a mess! The moving team had left and somehow, they had screwed everything up. I was in the car in 10 minutes and met Shawn in the lobby about 4:00 a.m. We pushed, pulled, lifted and organized the furniture according to the diagram. We were sweating and furious and we were also having fun. We knew this was going to be a HUGE day, and if it went well, it would set up the organization, as well as each of us for success. In addition, the two of us were now forever bonded over this experience.

Getting Executives to Produce

The executives came in a few hours later to an environment they didn't expect. Couches, loungers, coffee tables were in each of the areas we'd set up. Shawn did a masterful job that day of facilitating more than 100 execs through approximately eight activities, in what I call Shawn-in-the round. It was like a Def Leppard concert in the late 80s when they were on tour and had their stage in the middle.

Shawn's team and an extended team of us who had been through innovation training facilitated smaller groups. When all was said and done, the executives had created over 500 strategy ideas and at the end of the day, had narrowed them down to four within a single day. In one day, we firmly believe our executives had produced more strategies around the consumer than what most organizations do in three to five years. We, (the bigger we, not just Shawn and me) really kicked ass that day!

You might be saying, "Jeez, Steve, what the hell is up with this long introduction when most of the rest of the content is so short?"? First, I refer you to the initial paragraph that you obviously skipped over. I would also offer you this. It's important to understand a little bit of context where Shawn and I come from, particularly Shawn, since a majority of the content that follows is his. He's an amazing business partner and is dogged about helping organizations focus on the consumer. I am probably more of the realist and I do have a tendency to scare the shit out of him occasionally with my creativity and ability to ideate. And, you had to have just a small slice of our background so that some of this stuff makes sense.

About *The Power of YES!*
in Innovation

When we first thought about writing a book, we talked a great deal about what we wanted to convey to you, our reader. After many discussions, we both looked at each other and laughed — we hadn't really spoken with our colleagues and business partners about what might be interesting to them in the context of the work and experiences we've had over the past six to seven years. So, we set out and had several informal conversations to gather input from those most likely to want to read this book — our "target audience." Thank you to all our partners and colleagues who provided input and feedback and for shaping the focus of this first book in a series that we will be releasing over the next several years.

Many of our partners and colleagues stated that they wanted to better understand how we got to this point in our careers where saying "YES!" really started to payoff. To be honest, several of them had a hard time understanding how shifting your mindset could have the type of impact it has had on us, our partners, and the consumers we have impacted. We decided to start with the concept of saying YES! to the Power of Innovation and to share the mindset that led us to this point. We were also inspired by a post Shawn wrote a couple of years ago where he very publicly talked about saying YES! more in his professional and personal life.

The Origin Story: YES! Comes Alive

Two years ago, Shawn first wrote about the Power of YES! in Innovation. He was in the process of looking to advance his career and one day decided to say YES! to several options that opened a number of doors he'd never thought possible. Shawn's corporate career started in a fairly unconventional manner. Having worked as a minister of music prior to joining the Walt Disney Company, then making his way into the Healthcare space. A clear career path, right? Yeah, not so much. The more we talked to our business partners, consumers, and colleagues; however, we realized that a small minority of those folks had similar journeys. That being on a journey in this consumer-centered innovative world is less of a straight line. Eventually, you DO get to that spot where you know you are doing good work and as Shawn says, *"Innovation isn't work, innovation is a lifestyle!"*

Having said all that, putting your experiences on paper for others to read is both exhilarating and terrifying at the same time. And we both said YES! to doing this book; we felt that it was worth it to put ourselves out there as authentically as we could even if it meant sharing some of our less than successful ventures. We adopted the cliché/mantra "if it helps one person." And if it did, then it was worth the energy and effort to share this with you.

What's in It for You?

A better way to phrase it is "What do we want for you?" We know if you are either already in the innovation space or thinking about innovation, you must be emotionally as well as intellectually ready. To

💡 A NOTE FROM STEVE

We also thought a lot about the pain we have seen organizations struggle with over the years. The pain of investing millions of dollars into solutions no one used. The pain of measuring customer satisfaction as they continued to roll the rock uphill and NOT listen to their front-line employees who touch the customer every day. So many examples and only so much space to type.

Note that none of what we have witnessed as far as we know was done with malintent. Business is so busy that it is hard to slow down and ask if we really understand what the consumer wants. It takes courage because we believe if we hire all these smart people, and pay them a lot of money, shouldn't they know inherently what people want? Kind of but not really. You hire really smart people to get the job done and part of that job is defined by what consumers want, and more importantly, what they are willing to purchase. So keep on spending millions of dollars investing in what you think is right for the consumer, and then call us when that fails so we can introduce you to your consumer.

be honest, when you come to the end of an 18-hour day in a design sprint with four days left to go, that emotional component is as or possibly even more important than the intellectual component because it's what keeps you moving forward. We want to instill an aspect of the innovators mindset from our perspective that motivates you to want to get up and take on what can sometimes seem to be an insurmountable challenge of changing a culture, getting your executives out of their offices and on the street, and talking to your consumers. You see, you will hear NO! way more than you hear YES! and we implore you to keep on moving, to get past the NO! and find the YES!

What's in it for us? Well, we both get to accomplish a lifelong dream of sharing some of our experiences. We also felt this was a good way to reflect on the work we have done together and that continues to inspire us daily. It has been a magnificent reminder that it is worth it to say YES! as we build The Nason Group and focus on consumer-centered innovation.

And finally, if you stick with this book, you'll begin to understand how we (and hopefully you) can turn a mindset into a set of values that you can not only use to operate your day-to-day corporate world, but you can also apply to your personal life. We call these our consumer principles or values comprised of "Know Me, Surprise Me, and Make It Easy." We speak to these three principles in the work we do and how it has impacted our lives professionally and personally. So, yeah. Hang out with us for a while. We openly accept your feedback (see our contact information in the back of the book), and understand that this has been our experience around consumer-centered innovation. It's not an advice book, but can it help you? We think so. If you turn to the next page, you've already said YES! to giving us a shot, and we thank you for that opportunity.

SECTION 1

An Introduction to
The Power of YES! in Innovation

Welcome to *The Power of YES! in Innovation*. We have taken lessons garnered from our collective consumer innovation experiences to share our thoughts and learnings with you, our reader. Several years ago, we would have never thought to say YES! to this type of endeavor. We weren't truly listening to what we were teaching as part of our consumer innovation work. Fortunately for us, we decided to "eat our own cooking" and take on *The Power of YES! in Innovation*.

The first section explores what occurs when you say YES! to the power of innovation. You can learn about yourself as a leader, team member, and even as an organization as you begin to say YES! We share the results of what happens when you follow your passion and allow yourself to keep saying yes, and eventually harvest the rewards of focusing on consumer innovation.

A final tip before you jump into the pages of this book ... Know that it does *not* need to be read in chronological order. Check out the topics by skimming the table of contents, then move around to areas that interest you.

CHAPTER 1

Innovation is Not Work!
Innovation is a Lifestyle!

Every time I look back at the past year, I grow 10 years wiser! When I first realized this, I asked myself why I felt this way. Was it because of something that had taken place in my personal life? Was it the result of something that had happened to me professionally? Could it have just been life itself? The answer is YES! — to all the above!

I remember clearly, walking into a new job with one of the best people I have had the pleasure to know in my life. We had an enormous challenge before us — but we never doubted our ability to get the job done. We met and worked with talented, dynamic and compassionate individuals. During that experience, so many lives and an incredible business have been transformed.

One of the things that made this experience so exciting for me was that my leader, my friend, trusted me and had allowed me to move in a direction I had always wanted to go. We could focus on transforming a culture and a business model. However, the coolest part was witnessing people transform and take flight — how innovation became part of their creative DNA.

�‍ A NOTE FROM STEVE

I can attest to the amazing transformation I've seen in Shawn. He has taken on his career and "owned" it. When he walked in to take over a significant position in a company that was failing financially, it took guts. I also learned the power of loyalty — the good kind, not the kind where you drive over a cliff. I saw Shawn really come to life as a passionate leader who led by example and who was beginning to understand himself, and the world around him more deeply.

Saying YES! does mean saying NO! to those things that get in the way of the Power of Innovation. It means saying NO! to decisions only being made at the executive level. Saying NO! to handcuffing your customer support reps to the script. Saying NO! to projects or initiatives that aren't informed by the consumer or tested with the consumer. Saying NO! in these and other instances helps you better know what to say YES! to and better meets the needs of the customer and the organization.

I have learned more about who I am and what I want to do. Most importantly, I know what I do not want to do. I have learned the type of leaders I like to be around, and the kind of teams I like to be a part of — ones with:

» **Passion!**

» **Drive!**

» **Intensity!**

» **The Spirit to Learn!**

» **The Spirit to Fail!**

» **The Spirit to Live Life Fully!**

I witnessed people achieve what they did not imagine they could achieve. I saw them take flight when they did not believe they even knew how to fly. Together, we built a model of innovation that allowed us to not only do it as a job, but to live it, breathe it, and have fun with it.

What I Learned ...

I want to focus my learnings on how we measure success in innovation and the impact it has on teams. I stumbled across another innovator, Adam Malofsky, who has written about innovation as a lifestyle. Adam shared an article about innovation metrics in Forbes, "Innovation is a Lifestyle, Not a Bunch of Metrics." The industry is caught up on ROI (*Return on Investment*) but not on ROI (*Return on Innovation*.) The metrics around these two ROIs are very different. Return on Investment is all about the money. Return on Innovation is all about the people, the process, what you have learned, and sometimes about the money.

Now don't get me wrong. I started my journey as a corporate finance person. I understand the impact to the bottom and the top line. However, in innovation, this cannot be the primary focus — or you put shackles and chains on the innovators within your organization.

💡 A NOTE FROM STEVE

Shawn is absolutely right — everyone has the ability to learn the process of innovation; however, you have to commit to being vulnerable to know the consumer. You have to be good at taking a prototype to the consumer and having them tell you the iteration is a piece of crap. Instead of crying, you must smile and ask, " ... what would make this more useful for you?" or something of that nature. And if you are not an innovator at heart, there is an easy fix for that problem. Get your backside out of the chair you are sitting in and go talk to people in the building and on the street. You don't even have to talk about something at your workplace. Pick something you are interested in and just go talk to consumers.

"I see innovation as a lifestyle. If you're not doing it 100 percent of the time, as a part of your body and soul, it's hard to be truly innovative."

— Adam Malofsky —

Yes, and Amen! When you are a leader of innovation, you must provide space for people to breathe, for them to explore what change looks and feels like. I used to believe that everyone could be an innovator. Here is what I believe now: **Everyone has the ability to learn the process of innovation, but not everyone is an innovator at heart!**

What I Will Do ...

I am going to focus on living out Innovation as a Lifestyle! I will not focus solely on the business or the situation, but rather on the why we are doing what we are doing. As a leader, I am going to unleash the Power of YES! in Innovation by equipping my team and my client's teams to envision and do things they may not believe possible.

Adam went on to say, "Innovation is not a program. It's a life-long enterprise. It's a lifestyle." I could not agree more with him. As you read the short vignettes in this book, you will see how innovation has changed my life; it drives who I am today as a man, father, husband, and businessman.

What You Can Do ...

If you are an innovator — a person who believes wholeheartedly that innovation is a lifestyle — I encourage you to take time to focus and declutter the obstacles in your life or work that are preventing you from living an innovation-driven life. I know, it may not be easy, but get back to the things you love. Do what you do best!

Remember, Innovation is Not Work — Innovation Is a Lifestyle!

CHAPTER 2

The Power of YES! in Three Simple Steps

"Each day, I try to live the Power of YES! The power to give people the freedom to explore, test, and win. The power to let my children be all they want to be. The power to allow innovators the freedom to create what has never been created before, and most importantly, the power to say YES! to life."

When I wrote this, I had no idea the profound impact these words would have on me as a leader, executive, friend, husband, father, and overall person. These words become more and more important to me every day as I walk through life.

I'll share a brief story about the Power of YES! in my own life. I had the privilege to be a part of an organization as the Chief Transformation Officer. When the opportunity was presented to me, I could have said no. I knew the role would be hard and a challenge for me, but I also knew I could not run from it. So, I said YES — and in doing so, learned so much about my capabilities as a person, and equally as important, about my capabilities as a leader!

First, I learned that as a C-Suite Executive, my word and actions could empower a culture to change. I did not need to be the decision maker. I did not need to know everything. I did not have to be at every meeting. All I had to do was say the word, YES!

>> **YES! You Can Make That Decision!**

>> **YES! You Can Take That Risk!**

>> **YES! You Are Able to Do It!**

Second, as a leader, I learned that I have the ability to see talents and skills within associates that they may not be able see or that they may not have had the opportunity to share.

Eleanor Roosevelt said, "Never allow a person to tell you no who doesn't have the power to tell you yes."

Simple! Yet still hard for so many leaders. As a leader, we have the power to say no — but being able to say yes opens the door for engaging collaboration, opportunities for growth and the realizing of untapped potential.

Now, saying yes has it risks — but you cannot empower your organization, your team, and your associates unless you are willing to take the first step. By doing so, you will equip your teams with their own courage to say YES!

Lastly, I learned that saying yes doesn't always mean that I am right or that it is going to go the way I want it to go. I must provide my team members the ability to fail or take risks that I may not take myself. This means I must empower and support my teams to make decisions that may not necessarily be the ones I would make. As I worked with my teams over the past year, I did my best to get out of the way and provide the freedom for them to be their

A NOTE FROM STEVE

You are a leader regardless of title. You either lead people or yourself and the challenge is universal – what will you say no to that frees you up to say YES! to all of the possibilities at work and in your life?

Once you start either in your personal life or your professional life, it will become contagious. One small YES! and you will begin to see and feel yourself transform. This does not mean that you will become a "Yes Man or Woman." You will become someone who is open to the possibilities. You will begin to take small, incremental steps initially, and then find yourself taking leaps in both your personal and professional life.

best. In doing so, I empowered them to become better leaders and stronger team members.

What I Will Do with It ...

I am determined to live by the Power of YES! How? By following these three simple steps:

Y – Yes, I can! Yes, you can! Yes, we can! Yes, yes, YES! In all circumstances, opportunities or challenges, I will do my best to say Yes first!

E – Equip and empower all those around me to not only reach for their dreams but for the things they may feel are unattainable.

S – Succeed! There is a measure of success within every opportunity. Even if I fail, I learn and I move forward.

In following these three steps, I am fulfilling a dream of my own to write a book — THIS BOOK along with a website on the Power of YES!

What You Can Do ...

My challenge to you is simply this: Live by the Power of YES!

Challenge yourself! Using the three steps outlined above, you will begin to not only live by the Power of YES!, but also to learn where YES! can take you personally and professionally. Open your mind to learning through failure and thinking about big things you can say YES! to in your own life. Take a look at your life and all the small decisions you make daily — then ask yourself where you can choose to say YES! to larger, more complex opportunities.

CHAPTER 3

The Power of YES! – The Origin Story

I have taken the time to reflect on my own life and the anniversary of our family moving from Dallas to Cincinnati that started a new journey for all of us several years ago. Through this experience and reflection, I have come to realize the power of the word YES! in my own life.

» **Yes, I can!**

» **Yes, you can!**

» **Yes, we can!**

» **Yes, yes, YES!**

Now let me be clear. *I do not believe* in people or organizations creating a culture of proverbial yes men or women. What I do believe in is empowering a culture for those around you to have the freedom to say yes, and the freedom to fail even while saying YES!

Sir Richard Branson states, *"If someone offers you an amazing opportunity and you are not sure you can do it, say yes. Then learn how to do it later."*

In April of 2014, Susie Moore, a life coach and wellness expert wrote a blog post titled, "Nine Little Known Truths About the Power of YES!"

There are an infinite number of reasons to say no, but something is stirring the yes within you. Listen to this voice. Pay attention to your gut. Pay attention to your first instinct. When moving to Cincinnati and walking away from a great career, my family and I had to listen to the inner voice, the inner YES!

YES! Leads to More Doors of *Opportunity*

Saying no often closes these same doors. Why would we purposely close doors in our life? Why not look for every open door? This is a motto I live by every day. The career I have chosen in innovation is one about risk. I cannot be risk-adverse. I must look for the "thing" in the future that might be just a cracked door and walk through it, explore it, and learn from it.

Life is Short. Don't Ask Why, Ask Why Not?

Every day I work with consumers, guests, and colleagues and we talk, teach, and ask about the five "whys." When I think about asking *why not*, it is about getting to the truth — to the real meaning, and not just asking why. As a child, I asked my parents innumerable "why" questions and drove them crazy. Over the years, I was taught by them, by other adults, and even by some teachers to quit asking why. Now, the funny thing is, I get paid to ask people why for a living!

Each day I try to live the Power of YES! — the power to provide my team freedom to explore, test, and win; the power to let my children be all they want to be; the power to allow students the freedom to

💡 A NOTE FROM STEVE

Saying YES! can be emotionally and intellectually challenging. If you struggle with saying YES! asking "why not?" is another great way to help you break out from the daily grind and open yourself up to new opportunities.

When Shawn made the decision to move his entire family, I recalled a similar point in my life. It is on the edge of terrifying and you find yourself saying a lot of "what if ... ?" And most of those end up being on the negative side. The reason? It is hard to believe in yourself, that you have this new opportunity, that you can succeed. Well, that's all bullshit – you wouldn't have gotten the offer or even been considered for it. Now, commit!

A former colleague of mine moved to the U.S. and the intent was to move his family after they sold their house. By month two, I realized he was never going to make it and after nine months and not seeing his family, he left the job defeated. To this day, he regrets not moving his family over. You see, constraints like a house or a new opportunity are a way to be creative, to use the natural problem-solving ability we've had since the time we were not yet at the top of the food pyramid. That "gut" feeling is really data if you listen to neuroscientist, it's just in a different form and we often ignore it. Use it and commit to your YES!

create what has never been created before, and most importantly, the power to say YES! to life.

Yes, I can. Yes, you can. Yes, we can.

What You Can Do ...

Reflect on your life and those opportunities you took to say YES! What did you learn, how committed were you and what doors did it open? Look for opportunities to say yes both personally and professionally. For inspiration, talk to your loved ones, your boss, your mentor or coach, the person in line waiting to get their food, or your seat mate on an airplane about when they've said YES!

Seek out opportunities you can say yes to and learn from them as you step into the unknown.

Practice Being Uncomfortable

It's easy to say no and when you say yes, that's when things get real, quick! As you begin to say YES! *(remember — you don't want to be a yes man/woman)* take notice of the additional doors of opportunity it opens. Continue to say yes to those things that help you live the life you desire. Be okay with simply learning from those doors you entered that maybe weren't right for you at the time, but that you were courageous enough to step through.

Keep. Saying. YES!

CHAPTER 4

Owning Your Story! Sharing Your Story! The Power of Your Story!

Why should I share my story? This is a question I have asked myself numerous times in my life, and once again, over the past several weeks. It all started when a colleague and I journeyed to Dubai in January. We — Steve Junion, Myself and Dr. Yousef all had friends and family very concerned about the fact we were traveling to the Middle East (this took place one week after the inauguration of the new administration) — but we chose to make the journey without fear.

During the week in Dubai, we met some amazing human beings all on the same journey that we are on to help fix the healthcare system. I remember in one of our sessions, sitting in a room filled with executives from Egypt, Saudi Arabia, Qatar, Abu Dhabi, and Dubai. A statement was made to me, "Shawn, we do not hate your president. We just want to understand him." Isn't that what we all really want, to just be understood at times?

Now let me jump ahead to last week. I was asked to facilitate a session at a conference focused on hosting MBE/WBE (Minority or Women Owned Businesses) businesses and corporations working with them. I have to be honest! I went in with no set expectation that anything great was going to come out of this event. OH, was I wrong!

It was an incredible event both from a business and personal perspective. I met some truly inspiring people and heard many motivational stories. In all of that, again, it was a challenge to me. I kept hearing in my head, *Shawn, own it!* When the event concluded, I walked back to my room, drained both emotionally and physically — but so full of joy for what I had just experienced. I left that event forever changed, but most importantly, I left with many new friends.

What I Learned on This Journey!

I learned that I need to be proud of who I am and what I am. Now, let me explain. I am an extremely extroverted person (some say, too extroverted.) My wife tells me that I have a bigger than life personality — much like my mother! Who better to learn from? At the same time, I have a quiet inner voice that can, at times, be a bit scary. This aspect of my personality comes from my father! My father, was 100 percent Comanche Indian.

Grandparents & Great Grandmother

I can only imagine what he and my mother faced when they got married in the 1960s in Tucson, Arizona. I have been asked my whole life if I'm Hispanic. I am not. I am Native American and Caucasian. My Father was born in Texas and my mother in the mountains of Kentucky (GO BIG BLUE!!!)

I was raised in Arizona and have had the privilege of living all over our great country. I don't really understand racism or treating people differently because of their lifestyles. I was simply taught to love, respect, and treat all people the same way. I thank my parents for this

💡 A NOTE FROM STEVE

Much of what we do in our work is gather stories. However, too often, we forget about our own stories. Like Shawn, we have to embrace our own stories.

In order to understand and empathize with others, we must also have empathy and passion for our own story. We have to see the value we bring every day and then look to our colleagues and others for the value they bring. When we embrace our story and the stories of others, we not only build relationships and empathy, we build community.

perspective and my upbringing. It really has helped me be who I am today, and continues to help me become who I need to be.

In the world of business, I look different, act different, and in many cases, just outright scare people (maybe it's the blue or red hair) — but that is just fine! Many of them need it! They need to think differently and embrace others who think and act differently than they do. Our world is made up of incredible diversity! Now, more than ever, what we need is the spirit of inclusion! We need to love each other as we love ourselves! All lives, all people, no matter color, lifestyle choice, or walk of life — deserve to be loved!

What I Will Do!

Personally, I will stay true to myself. I will love all those I come into contact with just as I love myself. I will respect all for who they are no matter where they come from. Professionally, I will embrace my heritage. I will say I am proud to be a minority-owned business. And I will seek to help all of us on this journey!

What You Can Do!

I just ask you to do the same! Nothing more, nothing less!

"Diversity and Inclusion are About Giving Value to Every Human Being, no Matter Our Differences."

The Pursuit of One's Passion

I have spent much of my life in pursuit of my passion. I spent years as a musician, a pastor, a finance leader, and then a leader in innovation in corporate America. But none of these professions have fulfilled me completely or given me peace. Do not get me wrong! I would not change one thing about the path I have taken, because each of these experiences has made me who I am today:

> » **A husband.**

> » **A father.**

> » **A leader.**

> » **A friend.**

I have had many conversations with friends, colleagues, and even strangers about the idea of following one's passion. Over and over again, the conversations made me realize: I have lost what I am passionate about!

So, I had to ask myself the following questions:

> » **Why do I do what I do every day?**

» **Why do I get out of bed in the morning?**

» **Why does all this really matter?**

While searching for the answers to these questions, I realized that I have been misidentifying my passion.

💡 A NOTE FROM STEVE

Shawn is right when he states that his passion is relationships. Relationships are truly at the core of everything Shawn and I do in our work and in our personal lives. From personal experience, Shawn's mindset has helped me begin to put my family first, something that hasn't always happened. He knows relationships are keys to success and happiness whether it be at home or work.

As we have worked together at multiple companies, the relationships we've formed with our colleagues has been equally as important. When we go into organizations, we are asking our colleagues to be uncomfortable and take risks that some would never have considered. Without a relationship, and an "I have your back'" attitude, there is no reason to trust someone and nothing changes.

When you get relationships right, the work gets done. When you focus on the person and what they need, not the work, the work gets done. When you clear out the barriers for that person, the work gets done. When you "stop" doing stupid shit or forcing more instead of stopping more, work gets done.

It turns out my passion is not my profession, rather it's relationships. I love building powerful, close relationships. My passion is not meeting a goal, a deadline, or even some other outcome. My passion is seeing others experience similar "aha moments." I can't tell you how excited I get when I see someone have an epiphany something bigger and better is out there. I love when I help others discover and find their own passions.

So where does innovation fit into this passion? Innovation is part of it. In working in innovation, I have the opportunity to partner with diverse people from all walks of life who share their unique experiences with me. It continually allows for "aha moments." Every day, I get to work with people whose lives are changed forever, because they continue to pursue their own passions and are creating something no one else has before.

Through this process, I discovered the answers to my questions:

> **People are why I do what I do every day.**

> **People are why I wake up in the morning.**

> **People matter. The people I talk to and build relationships with every day matter. The people who are out there imagining new things and who are changing the world one idea at a time matter.**

I was sitting at a table with a group of diverse leaders when I witnessed passion at its best. I saw a colleague stand-up for everything she believed in, namely for the one-thing she was passionate about. What was truly amazing to me was that she did not back down from her belief even when others questioned it. It greatly impacted my life. It showed me to stand, to believe, and to live for it all, no matter the cost!

How Do You Find Your Passion? Warren Berger, wrote an article titled, "Find Your Passion with These Eight Provoking Questions." The questions he asks force you to think outside your comfort zone. They compel you to accurately identify your passion. Additionally, I use a great tool, the Passion Planner, that helps me properly identify and keeps me on my "passion" track. The Passion Planner is the life coach that fits into your backpack, briefcase, or purse. It allows you to create your passion plan and your path to get there.

What You Can Do ...

Ask yourself the three questions listed above EVERY day for the next month. Once you have begun to focus on what's important for you, I encourage you to find time and to take time to focus on the one thing you are passionate about — the one thing that is going to allow you to focus on what you truly love to do.

Find Your Passion! Chase Your Passion! Live Your Passion!

So, what's your passion?

CHAPTER 5

Where Has the Consumer Gone?

Over 175,000 people ascend on the Las Vegas Strip each January to see the coolest and newest technologies. I mean, who doesn't love drones choreographed to the Macarena or a personalized hair coach embedded in a hair brush? Or, the amazing new Sleep Number 360 smart bed?

I had the honor to sit on a panel for the Digital Health summit and to moderate a panel during the TransformingEDU Summit. As I moved between both ballrooms, I heard innovators and industry leaders within healthcare share innovations around attacking cancer, conquering chronic conditions and even one company, Omron Healthcare, has a "moonshot" for zero heart attacks or strokes.

I then looked at connected health, artificial intelligence, and how messaging will be the backbone of healthcare connectivity. In education, I witnessed how virtual reality and augmented reality could change the education experience.

Now, these are incredible ideas, but I could not help but wonder if this exciting maker movement is a trend, a fad — or is it here to stay? I had witnessed these amazingly cool things, but I kept asking myself one question:

Where Has the Consumer Gone?

Why was I asking myself that question? I wasn't sure, but then at dinner that night, a colleague of mine asked the same question.

... if the consumer is not involved in creating it, testing it, and using it — it is nothing more than technology.

Here is my learning: We have amazing, life-changing technology both in the wings and in the marketplace — however, *if the consumer is not involved in creating it, testing it, and using it — it is nothing more than technology.* The value in technology is at its highest when it is inextricably linked with the consumer experience.

Further, the correlation of healthcare to the education industry is mind-blowing. The biggest question I ask is, when will we treat students like a consumer and not as second-class citizens? Educators need to understand who is paying the bill. In April of 2016, an article was written about the Ed Tech Cool Down, that it had reached an all-time low from an investment place. I am anxious to see where the year ended.

What's My Takeaway?

This is simple! What I am going to do is to keep saying, YES!

Yes, to innovation! Yes, to the consumer! Yes, yes, YES!

I will listen to the consumer! I will spend more time with consumers, patients, and members! I will take time to hear their story. Remember

💡 A NOTE FROM STEVE

CES is truly an amazing "show" hosted by a city that really knows how to put on a good presentation. I was that colleague with Shawn and in all but one or two panels, presentations, etc., the consumer was non-existent. How can that be?

Is it the allure of technology? Technology IS sexy and there are billions of dollars being poured into advancing technology, but at what cost? Remember technology is being used by a significant amount of doctors and nurses, and they sometimes despise the technology. Why? It wasn't designed with them in mind. It is hard to use. They feel pissed off because they spend more time fighting technology versus talking to patients.

This experience fueled Shawn and I to make a commitment to listen more deeply. We committed to telling our consumers' stories to those people who matter and who can make a difference in the lives of those they serve. We committed to helping organizations really know their consumer because it is why we exist in this current iteration. To all of this, we say YES!

this, we are all humans. We all have a story to tell — regardless of industry, and we must involve the consumer in everything we do.

From the beginning to the end of the process: We need everyone's voice. I have said it numerous times in my blog. Know Me! Surprise Me! Make It Easy! Focus on this and we will all win!

What You Can Do ...

Spend time with your customer, consumer, patient or member!

Go. Now.

CHAPTER 6

"Run, Forrest, Run!" – Running Ahead of Your Bullies

A powerful scene in the movie, *Forrest Gump*, occurs when Jenny and Forrest walk down the dirt road and three bullies show up. Do you remember what happens next? The three bullies begin throwing rocks at Forrest; one even pings off his forehead. At first, Forrest did not know what to do. Then Jenny, his best friend in the whole-wide-world, looked at him and said, "Run, Forrest, run!"

When Forrest began to run, it was not pretty. As a matter of fact, it was downright pitiful. He was running down that dirt road in braces with nowhere to go. But he did not give up. He kept running as fast as he could to get away from the bullies. Before you know it, the braces started to break and fall off — much like shackles being removed from a prisoner. FORREST WAS FREE!

He could not only run, but he could run fast — and he outran the bullies — becoming stronger in the process!

What I Learned ...

The moral of that scene is much like many of our experiences
in the world of innovation. We find ourselves faced with bullies

 A NOTE FROM STEVE

Consumer-Centered Innovation is probably both the most
amazing as well as the ugliest process I have been involved
with in the corporate world.

It is amazing when people see the results. It is amazing when
individuals and leaders see they don't need to have all the
answers. It is amazing to see how their consumers react to
their ideas and prototypes. The challenge is that we typically
have to walk through the ugliness, to get to this amazing
place where leadership, in particular, can see the Power of
YES! in Innovation!

Ugliness comes in all forms. It comes in the form of
top-down-structures and decision-making. It comes in the
form of my turf vs. your turf. It comes in the form of not
being willing to have my team participate cross-functionally
because we have our shit together and you don't. My truth?
Those are all bullshit responses. Even if you do know your
consumer, by not participating, you are sub-optimizing the
rest of the performance of the organization. By not shifting
your mindset, you are inviting your competition to eat your
lunch and take your consumers away from you.

Be like Forrest, break free from those mindsets that limit you!

— sometimes from the outside — but many times from within our walls. People are often afraid of the unknown. They fear that they might mess-up or worse, they might fail.

I was asked about running ahead — and if there were anything I would do differently in my approach to innovation within the two industries – healthcare and higher education — that need INNOVATION. Here is my response:

> » **No, I wouldn't do anything different!**

> » **Run fast, run without fear!**

What I Will Do ...

As a man, father, husband, and leader, I have made a conscious and challenging choice to let people run! I came across a page on LifeHack.org titled, "Run, Forrest, Run! 16 Life Lessons We Can Learn from Forrest Gump." As I read through it, I found that many of the points highlighted need to be part of our innovation toolkit. Here are six I believe are key:

> › Don't Be Afraid to Be Honest – If we are willing to be honest, we may be able to come to the right solution sooner than later.

> › Don't Be Afraid to Lose (Fail) – Fail Fast, Fail Forward! Just Do It!

> › Always Try New Things. You Might Be Great at Them – If we do not try new things, everything will always be the same. That is not Innovation!

> › Sometimes, You Just Have to Do the Right Thing – Even When Everyone Tells You Not To

> › Remember, we all are humans. We all are consumers. Do what is right!

> › You Never Know Whose Lives You'll Change — Exactly!

💡 A NOTE FROM STEVE

Stepping into the unknown takes courage. You could be the first one to take the risk and you will feel the eyeballs of everyone watching to see if you succeed or fail. And, when you take that first step like many of our colleagues have, it will free you from many of the ideas that have tied you down. Many people will say my leader won't let me do [insert thing] or the culture punishes people who step out of bounds. Sure, some of that may be true, but what's truer is that if you keep making stuff up in your head, you'll find yourself in a daily grind instead of a career you love.

Failing is learning. The process we take people through encourages failure, especially up front. As we work with teams and we all become more informed by the consumer and our increased knowledge, failure becomes harder to actually accomplish! There is a method to the process that many of our partners and colleagues find freeing. Sometimes you'll hear us saying, "freedom within a framework". As leaders, we must provide this framework to our colleagues.

The Power of YES! is about finding connections between your values and work. It begins with you, along with support from your leader and colleagues. You have to be able to see and translate how what you do has meaning and impact even if you are far removed from the customer. The key is that it starts with you.

So, go for a run! Do the thing that is on top of your mind but that you have been afraid to do. Go. Now.

> Do What You Love — Why would you do anything else?

What You Can Do ...

It is all about RUNNING! It is all about taking ACTION! We, as innovators, know what needs to be done, but what matters the most is that we — RUN!

I encourage you to take 30 minutes and do something you have been afraid to do. Go have fun! Go learn something new! Break free!

CHAPTER 7

Design-Led Strategy:
The New Strategy for Tomorrow!

Over the past ten years in my career, I have had the privilege to meet with hundreds if not thousands of consumers from all walks of life. In this journey, I have focused primarily on well-being and what we could do to enhance one's well-being. I have come to one conclusion: WE CAN'T! All we can do is create a journey where we KNOW THEM, SURPRISE THEM, and MAKE IT EASY FOR THEM!

I have traveled all across this country and I've heard the same thing over and over, *Are you listening to me?* And frankly, for years, no- we were not. Over the past year my passion to have empathy for every person, no matter what stage in the journey one is on has grown.

So What? You Might Be Asking?

What does all of this have to do with strategy? Everything. I read an article by Lee Comber titled, "Why Design-Led Companies Do Better in Business." You can read the full article, but I want to point out the four imperatives he talks about:

The Purpose is the Brief – Make your strategy simple. Make sure your colleagues and consumers can understand it. Simple, simple, simple!

Craft the Whole Experience – Using design at the core of your business will ensure success. Change your operational model. Flip your way of thinking. Put design and the consumer in the middle before you ever focus on the bottom line.

Design for the On-Demand Age – Be nimble! Be quick! Do not take anything for granted. Make sure your strategy can change on a dime, but not change who you are as a business.

Simplify and Seduce – I have to go back to one of my favorite Steve Jobs quote for this.

> *"Simple can be harder than complex: You have to work hard to get your thinking clean to make it simple, but it's worth it in the end because once you get there, you can move mountains."*
>
> — Steve Jobs —

What You Can Do ...

» **Love your consumer!**

» **Appreciate your colleagues!**

» **Keep things simple!**

» **And create a kick-ass strategy that is focused on all of them!**

💡A NOTE FROM STEVE

I can't believe we've made it this far in the book, if you are reading chronologically, without our Steve Job's quote. I am so sick of seeing this quote and yet, it wouldn't feel right NOT having it in this book.

As many times as I see it, it truly is the hardest thing for humans, as a species, to do! Simplicity really does cut at the core of what most consumers want. In this high-stress, highly-distracted world we live in, those brief moments of simplicity often surprise us. Comments like "That's all I have to do?" Or, "That's it, you don't need anything else?" are the dream of many consumers. Each of us have stories like this; however, there are typically more stories about how much a pain in the ass an experience was. Don't believe me? Look at your Facebook or Twitter feed. How much of what is going on in those feeds concerns someone who has had a bad experience vs. a good experience?

No, We Can't Do It!

"No, we can't do it!" This is a common phrase I have heard in my years as a leader in innovation. From big organizations to small ones, from the government to education. It seems it is easier for people to say no, instead of YES!

A team I worked with reminded me again what it means to have RESILIENCE. Resilience is the ability to become strong, healthy, or successful again after something bad happens. In my world, many times that is focused on failure or the failure of a new idea, solution, product, or service.

As I look back on my experiences, there have been times where resilience was the only thing that got me through what I was doing. I had to have a mindset that nothing would distract me from the purpose or mission in front of me. I am not going to lie; innovation is not for the faint of heart. It is for the person who is willing to take those biggest challenges, opportunities, or frontiers not yet explored and go after them.

Resilience: The ability to become strong, healthy, or successful again after something bad happens.

8 STEPS TO BECOME MORE RESILIENT

1
Accept change
Find ways to become more comfortable with change.

2
Become a continuous learner
Learn new skills, gain new understanding and apply them in times of change.

3
Take charge
Take charge of your own career and your own development.

4
Find your sense of purpose
Helps you to assess setbacks within the framework of a broader perspective.

8
Skill shift
Reframe how you see your skills, talents and interests.

7
Reflect
Reflection fosters learning, new perspectives and self-awareness.

6
Cultivate relationships
Develop and nurture a broad network of personal and professional relationships.

5
Pay attention to self-identity
Form your identity apart from your job.

Center for Creative Leadership

What I Will Do ...

In my travels, I viewed this infographic published by The Center For Creative Leadership titled "Eight Steps To Become More Resilient." I realized it really did come back to simply saying, YES!

» **Yes, I will accept change!**

» **Yes, I will learn!**

» **Yes, I will take charge of my destiny!**

» **Yes, I will find my sense of purpose!**

» **Yes, I will be me!**

» **Yes, I will have relationships!**

» **Yes, I will reflect!**

» **Yes, I will shift!**

A NOTE FROM STEVE

There are a number of apps released to increase resiliency. Why pay for an app, when life can be your app? To build up resilience, the eight steps pointed out are great *and* involve you taking the first step. They involves doing one thing every day differently until you realize it has become a part of your habits to do things differently. It involves taking care of yourself (mind, body, and soul.) Most importantly, by saying YES! you open yourself up to making major shifts professionally and personally.

What I Learned ...

This is truly the essence of the Power of YES! in Innovation! You must say yes to yourself some mornings when you get up, or when you walk into that meeting where you know you are going to face opposition. You must have RESILIENCE!

What You Can Do ...

Focus on the eight steps to becoming more resilient. Say, YES! first, then take action!

CHAPTER 8

How to Climb Mt. Bold Without Giving Up

There are days when climbing Mt. Bold just seems impossible. You ask, what is Mt. Bold? For you Mt. Bold may be dealing with a boss or a job. For a friend, Mt. Bold may just be coping with children and a partner. For a stranger, Mt. Bold may have just walked by, driven by, sat by or it may just be facing their day-to-day life.

So, what is my Mt. Bold? It is learning that although I can see clearly how innovation can transform education, healthcare, and individual lives, not everyone else does (or even wants to.) It is learning that in the face of adversity there are still a million more victories to stand tall about. I have been reading a book called *Bold*, by Peter H. Diamandis and Steven Kotler. The book has been instrumental in helping me shape my thinking and change mindsets that I have allowed to cloud my judgment. For example:

> » **Shawn, you can't change a system!**

> » **You can't make this work.**

> » **You are moving too fast!**

» **Is all this innovation stuff just fluff?**

NO!

In fact, what I am trying to do is dare to be different and not allow NO! to be told as a final answer. As a matter of fact, Diamandis and Kotler give a great rule to follow in the book, "No, simply means begin one level higher!"

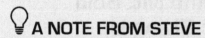

A NOTE FROM STEVE

You most certainly want like-minded people who want to change the system, move fast, etc. You also want people to challenge your thinking and to help you get there faster.

I'm not speaking of people who want to disagree for the sake of disagreeing but of people who help to take your thinking to the extremes. Innovation is not the brilliance of one person, but the culmination of sparks and building upon others' observations, insights, and talents.

When you surround yourself with people who have a purpose and challenge each other, NO! begins to disappear from the culture. It is replaced by "how" questions. How might we [insert idea here]? How does this support our existing and future customers? How does this impact our business model?

"The day before anything is truly a breakthrough, it's a crazy idea. Right? So where are we trying crazy ideas?"

— Peter Diamandis —

Diamandis states, "The day before anything is truly a breakthrough, it's a crazy idea. Right? So where are we trying crazy ideas?" Where are you trying crazy ideas? My crazy idea is that I truly believe we can transform major systems and business models that have not been touched in 500+ years into something new and powerful. How, you might ask? By being BOLD! I refuse at this point in my life to allow anyone to hold me down, hold me back, or to tell me it can't be done.

So, how do we do this? How do we climb Mt. Bold without giving up? We surround ourselves with like-minded people who possess the same determination not to quit! Sometimes, you need people who just have the courage to stand-up with you and climb the mountain.

One of the things Diamandis and Kotler encourage is to create your own set of laws or rules to live by. Here are some of those rules, known as Peter's Laws:

- » **When given a choice – take both!**
- » **Do it by the book – but be the author!**
- » **If you can't win, change the rules.**
- » **Don't walk when you can run.**
- » **The faster you move, the slower time passes, the longer you live.**
- » **If you think it is impossible, then it is for you.**

You don't have to use only the ones you have come up with. Steal, tweak, and rearrange ones others use. Here are the Nine Principles for Innovation Google lives by:

> Innovation comes from anywhere

> Focus on the user

> Aim to be 10 times better

> Bet on technical insights

> Ship and iterate

> Give employees 20 percent of time

> Default to open processes

> Fail well

> Have a mission that matters

I have done a lot of reading and thinking on what my principles, laws, or rules to live by are going to be. I still have not come up with what I feel are right for me. However, I continue to work on it daily.

What You Can Do ...

Take some time, find a quiet place and reflect on how you will climb Mt. Bold without giving up! What are the principles, values, laws and/ or mantras you will use to power through those challenging times — professionally and personally? Write them down, give them a name, and put them into practice daily.

CHAPTER 9

What I Thought I Knew –
I Learned at "The Network"

The Story ...

This past week, Steve and I traveled to Boston to attend the inaugural Innovation Leader event, The Network! There were 50 innovators and disruptors from all industries and walks of life. Now, let me be perfectly honest — most in the room were at one time involved in corporate innovation and frankly had gotten sick of all the red tape and bureaucracy.

Additionally, many of us in the room are in some type of consultant role. I wasn't sure what to expect but it turned out to be AWESOME! We met some incredibly cool people and made new friends that in the future, I know we will turn to for their rich knowledge and expert skills.

One of those crazy people was Toni Newman. Toni is a ROCK STAR who is passionate about the architecture and dynamics of consumer experience. I love Toni's favorite saying, "Why Not!"

This story is just one of the many that we heard during the day. I look forward to getting together again. Thank you, Innovation Leader!

What We Learned and What You Can Learn ...

Innovation Failure – 97 percent of executives or CEO's are unhappy with their innovation work in Corporate America. The discussions in the room that day were rich — so many execs present had experienced failure and felt unhappy. The interesting thing is that FAILURE is at the heart of Innovation. It's what you do with it that makes the difference in attitude and value. Unfortunately, many of these teams are just applying innovation for innovation's sake, instead of tying it to their business goals.

Just recently, I read a blog from Phil McKinney, The CEO of Innovation Dilemma. Phil states that 97 percent of CEOs say innovation is important, Seventy-three percent agree it's important in their organization, but only 35 percent are confident their organization can do it. So, what do we do?

Storytelling – What is your desired ending? What is your controlling idea? How Can I Build Empathy? What Is My Innovation Story?

Think about these three things

> Act One: What is the Challenge?

> Act Two: What is the Struggle?

> Act Three: What Changed in the World?

Each of us in this space has a story connecting us to our consumers. Some of them good, some of them not so good. But the bottom line is that we all have a narrative around our journey and our experiences. Learn how to share your story. People and/or consumers respond with richer engagement and loyalty when they can connect to who you are.

Landscape Scan – At the end of the day at THE NETWORK, we did an exercise to examine the Innovation Landscape, which was led by

---

💡 A NOTE FROM STEVE

Toni is absolutely crazy in the most amazing way! She is worth the follow on Twitter and/or her TED Talk or anything she does. What I love about her the most is that she has no fear. Everyone is her friend, and she has an amazing story!

In addition, I have made a career out of failure, I mean learning. I have at least one conversation a week about what it means to fail and how failure is important from a personal and professional perspective to growth.

Innovation fails, I believe, because we don't allow individuals in an organization to have a mindset that failure is learning. Instead, the culture and leaders punish frequently those going outside the boundaries or guard rails that have been used in corporate CYA.

As leaders, it is important to provide cover for our colleagues and associates to learn. We have to enable them to explore and learn and grow. Not everyone is a Toni, but I bet Toni would be the first to tell you to walk into the unknown and the fear. When you come out on the other side, you may be scarred a bit, but you will be so much more knowledgeable and comfortable with yourself.

Dave Rutley and his team from Collective Next. We started with 2017 and looked back 10+ years and forward 10+ years. It was a powerful exercise witnessing the think tank in the room. Here are a couple of quick highlights the group came up with:

Thought Leadership – The people and influencers we currently look to are shifting, yet we still depend a great deal on the founding leaders of this movement.

Methodologies – These come and go, but what doesn't change is there is always a consumer!

Landscape – Things are moving so fast in the world today that we as innovators are challenged to keep up more than ever before.

What We Can Do and What You Can Do ...

This is pretty simple! Keep learning! Keep partnering! Keep exploring! As I stated above, the world is changing at an incredible pace. You must stay ahead of challenges and obstacles so you can continue to INNOVATE!

Take 15 minutes this week. Get out and do something new and different. Challenge yourself to get out of the norm!

SECTION 2

Leading Through
The Power of YES! in Innovation

Leadership is critical to ensuring that the organization can fully realize the impact of the Power of YES! in Innovation. In this section, we will explore some of the principles that we believe in and that have helped us develop organizations focused on consumer-innovation. Not always easy, but always worth it.

› Leaders must be able to lead as generalists and be comfortable extending their leadership into areas outside their domain. Mark Burnett stated, "Specialists have jobs. Generalists build empires!"

› Leaders need to see the big vision for transformation and empower their organization to engage in new ways of thinking, working, and communicating.

› Leaders need to create the space to fail and learn. It's not about celebrating failure just for the sake of failing, but failure and learning incorporated into the next iteration of the service or product.

› Leaders, don't run so fast that you leave everyone behind.

💡 **A NOTE FROM STEVE**

The Power of YES! in Innovation begins with leadership. If you start with mindset, you have motivated groups without support and resources. If you have a culture of innovation, new leadership can quickly come in and destroy that culture with a new mindset. It starts with leadership and the ability to allow your colleagues to bring their whole selves to work every day. It requires new competencies, skillsets, and most importantly, mindset.

Consumer-centered innovation is all about transformation and transformation can be daunting for colleagues, leaders, and the entire organization. Transformation requires and results in incredible disruption — and leaders need to be outstanding at communicating common, consistent messages about how the transformation will enable the company to meet the needs of their consumer and how everyone's role can contribute. The only way you can improve your consumer's experience and build up your brand loyalty is by embracing change (disruption) and keeping your eye on the consumer. Leading the kind of transformation to a consumer-centered innovation culture isn't easy. It requires knowledge, skills, and abilities beyond those of more traditional leaders.

Leading consumer-centered innovation requires leadership to give permission space for people to fail, which we will discuss in this section. Previous cultural norms and leadership models did NOT allow people to fail and were punitive for those stepping outside of the cultural boundaries. What does it mean for those organizations where individuals are not allowed to fail? Nothing. And that's just one of the greatest challenges as you transition and infuse consumer-centered innovation into an organization, getting people to make decisions and giving them permission to take risks and to fail. Leading organizations in the middle of this type of transformation means that you want to build a culture that encourages colleagues to go out to experiment, to fail and build a buzz around the organizations.

The mantras of the innovation leader range from "Fail fast, fail forward" or one of our favorites from Marcus Shingles, "You must fail to have disruptive innovation!" It's all about Fast Learning. Fail forward and learn. Don't just fail and celebrate."

CHAPTER 10

Creating a Magical Experience! How You Go from Finance to Consumer-Centered Innovation!

I get asked frequently, "Shawn, how did you get into innovation and consumer experience?" My journey is probably not much different than many of us who work in the industry. You are doing one thing one day, and then the next day you want to do something different. I had spent the first part of my career as a musician, and was living in Orlando. My wife and I are huge Disney fans, so I took a leap and applied for a finance position (because that is a logical jump), and I got it.

Over the next six years, I had an incredible journey. I worked with extraordinary cast members, learned a great deal, and even worked with the Disney Cruise Line. Let me be clear! Disney has a culture of innovation. You begin to find yourself thinking differently — looking at things from a new perspective and ultimately, crafting business decisions differently. In the final part of my journey at Disney, I had the honor to become a Walt Disney Imagineer — an experience that transformed me.

WOW! What a journey it was! It was an incredible time in my life. I got to do CONSUMER-CENTERED INNOVATION Disney style. I learned two things that changed the course of my life.

First, I learned I hated finance!

Second, I learned there is no price tag on creating an experience for your guest, customer, or consumer!

 In this two-minute video, I share some of my thoughts around embracing innovation and creating a premium consumer experience. Scan the code on the left from your phone to watch the video.

(https://videopress.com/v/SyLtLKFa)

As I stated above and shared in the video, there is no price to creating a premium experience for your consumer — whether it be your end-user, a stakeholder, or the person sitting next to you. This idea has become such a passion of mine over the past five years, and I am determined that we can disrupt industries that do not do this well.

An article by, Steve Towers, is titled, "The Five Crucial Things Successful CX companies Do Every Day." Steve states the following in his article:

> Top teams understand CX success and move out of the way of their people to let them get on with it.

> Customer needs are understood and developed to create the organizational alignment toward successful customer outcomes.

> Being customer-centric isn't about projects. It is a state of mind.

> Successful CX transcends measures and implements a rigorous feedback/feed forward framework.

› CX is both the strategy and the operational objective to overcome needless complexity.

What I Learned ...

You must take ground. Although I do not know if I agree with Steve's top five, I do agree you must start somewhere. That somewhere is with your consumer not only in the center of what you do but throughout their entire journey! Involve them like never before! As I work with partners, I'll continue to put the consumer in the middle of everything we do, and I will help organizations develop empathy for the entire journey of the consumer in using their product or service.

A NOTE FROM STEVE

Diversity is key. Not only the big "D" but the little "d" in diversity. From an innovation perspective, we see the little "d" in diversity in terms of diversity of background, of thoughts, education and life experiences. Working in a CCI environment means that you are working with consumers and customers. They have to be able to relate to you.

Diversity in career paths is also important. The breadth that is important in leadership is also important for individual contributors focused on innovation. The more diverse an individual and teams' experience, the more robust will be the perspective of the consumer.

What You Can Do ...

Today, I leave you with this thought: What are you doing for your consumer? Are you focused on them in everything you do? It is not always easy, and sometimes it can be challenging. Take 30 minutes and do the following:

1. **INSIGHTS:** Research three companies that are consumer-centered and are known for their experiences (Nordstrom, Disney, Amazon, Marriott, Delta, etc.)

2. **INITIATE:** Write down what it is that sticks out to you about those experiences.

3. **IDEATE:** Think out of the box! Create potential ideas, solutions, or products to create experiences within your business.

CHAPTER 11

"The Good, the Bad, and the Ugly" of Innovation

As an executive, one thing I have learned to do is run fearlessly. When leading radical change around consumer innovation, don't be concerned about what the organization is doing or you will get bogged down in the past and why something can't be done versus moving the organization forward.

As a leader, you need to be fully aware that by running fast, you will significantly impact the culture. As you are running, you need to assess the current culture and how it can support consumer-driven innovation, or more importantly, throw up barriers that impede the kind of culture needed to support this kind of innovation while creating a new culture. This was the case in my previous position where I was the Chief Transformation Officer, and we broke every change management rule, strategy, and playbook. We simply didn't have time. The platform was already in ashes, and we needed to put the organization on the path toward profitability by focusing on the consumer.

I've always believed, and for most of my career have lived with, the mantra of "bringing your whole self to work"! What does that mean?

💡 A NOTE FROM STEVE

The good focuses and articulates clearly the "why." The good has high expectations and instills the desire to achieve results. The good enables the "how" because innovation requires a level of collaboration across the organization. The customer is not only impacted when they have a concern and call customer service; they are impacted by many of the decisions made across the organization before the customer ever purchases the product or service.

The good focus relentlessly on knowing the consumer and their customers. They never have it all figured out. They are constantly asking new questions, testing new hypotheses and incorporating their insights across the organization.

The good focuses on leadership that enable their colleagues to achieve the unthinkable. It's not just about breaking down barriers as a leader. It's about building the capabilities, cultivating the mindset, and most importantly, building the next generation of innovation leaders by giving individuals and teams the space to experiment, fail, learn and to repeat the cycle.

It means that I bring my real, authentic self as a leader as well as a follower to the organization. What matters are results, not that I have red or blue hair or earrings or anything else.

Leading by example and giving people the space to just be themselves is powerful in creating an organization that can relate to consumers. As an executive, I saw that one of my primary roles was to allow colleagues to think differently and be free, allowing the creative in each person to be seen and appreciated.

This is a great place to start when building an effective, consumer-focused culture. It's not the end, and throughout each step, your colleagues, peers, and leadership will be watching. They will be watching to see if you truly believe in allowing people to bring their whole selves to work. Ask yourself these questions:

> Do you focus on results or the proverbial dress code?

> Do you focus on building the culture where it is safe to take risks and fails?

> What happens the first time someone fails on a large scale?

> How do you react? Do people get punished, or do we look at "failures" as a learning opportunity?

Implementing deep change means that as a leader, you must effect change and build the culture that can meet the consumers where they are at, not where you think they are.

What I Will Do with It ...

I'll keep running fearlessly and enable those I lead to do the same. I will continue to learn the difference between creating a culture focused on the consumer versus one that destroys the morale of my colleagues. I will allow every person under my purview to bring their whole selves to work and make sure that everyone is accepted for the results they create, not the way they look.

What You Can Do ...

Run with a passion and fearlessness to say you are going to make change. Be clear about the expected result (outcome) and allow your colleagues and organization to find the path (the process.) They may need insights into the process, but the playbook changes based on the previous culture and the needs of colleagues to move into that creative space that wants to focus on the consumer. In the end, make sure that you and your colleagues just focus on doing cool shit that matters.

CHAPTER 12

Failure ... Deal with It!

"Anyone who says failure is not an option has also ruled out innovation."

— Seth Godin —

One of the greatest basketball players of all time, Michael Jordan talks about how his great success is due to the fact he learned how to fail. Jordan said, *"I've missed more than 9,000 shots in my career. I've lost almost 300 games. Twenty-six times, I've been trusted to take the game-winning shot and missed. I've failed over and over, repeatedly in my life. And that is why I am succeeding."*

Thomas Edison talked about his success this way, *"I have not failed. I've just found 10,000 ways that won't work."*

Apple great, Steve Jobs wasn't afraid to fail, and once said, *"The greatest artists like Dylan, Picasso, and Newton risked failure. And if we want to be great, we've got to risk it, too."*

Why Failure? Why Not?

Running an Innovation Organization can be challenging at times, especially when we start talking about failure. Our traditional higher education and corporate systems do not give permission, space, or opportunities for students to fail.

I had a conversation with the CEO and co-founder of the innovative start-up that is transforming how young people search for and find their career and life's passion. While the CEO was talking about their own career and their path to the start-up, they put it this way, *"I failed … before I succeeded."*

> *" … we must provide a safe place and environment for everyone to fail, so they can learn from their mistakes, learn how to bounce back, and ultimately learn to succeed."*

Now, I am not saying by any means that our students should fail a class or fail-out of college or that colleagues should fail so badly they should be exited from the organization. What I am saying is, we must provide a safe place and environment for everyone to fail, so they can learn from their mistakes, learn how to bounce back, and ultimately learn to succeed.

Colleagues need to learn the system of innovation — the process. They need to learn not everything they do will come out perfectly on the first try. They need to learn they can't just give up when things don't go their way or even how they had hoped. They need to learn there are infinite possibilities and even more discoveries awaiting them every single time they fail. As leaders, we are here to let others fail! Because, we believe there is no better way to innovate than in a place that is safe to grow, discover, fail, and try again.

Failure in Innovation!

There are three critical steps for harnessing failure in innovation. First, you need to launch your project. Don't worry about not knowing everything yet; you will get there in the second step. If you have an idea or a concept, use that as your starting point. The second step is to build and refine through iteration. In many cases, when we work with customers, we have them building and refining artifacts that describe their customers — for example, personas and journey maps during their first exposure to design thinking types of tools. Every two weeks, we expect our customers to iterate, build, and present to the team their progress and current iteration. The last step is to embed the learning, and this begins by breaking down the wall of perfection. Because we have our customers building initial drafts the first day we launch products, we immediately begin to incorporate the concept of "fail fast, fail cheap." We also embed the learning that comes from those initial drafts through a process of reflection.

When I advise the communities, I tell them this: Release, release, release! Get your project, service, or idea out. Don't worry about failure. Failure is how we learn. Alpha, Beta, Release ... 30 percent done, (figure out and fix what's not working) 60 percent done, (figure out and fix whatever else isn't working), 100 percent done! (Be prepared to keep working)! Each of these steps, each of these failures, gets you to success.

Additionally, we advise that you need to be first to market! It doesn't have to be perfect. It just has to get out there. Learn from the first release and re-release. Learn from each failure. You will always fail, so deal with it!

What I Learned ...

The more I encouraged people to fail, the more they learned, and the faster those learnings were incorporated into the product, service, or operations of the organization. The more I encouraged people to fail, the bolder the organization got in terms of thinking about how to better focus on the consumer. The more I encouraged failure, the better results we got as an organization.

What You Can Do ...

Prepare for and expect failure!

Change your mindset, language and intention from "I'm failing" to "I'm learning!" This is the biggest shift you can make for yourself in your personal and professional life. This seemingly simple change, once you not only begin to believe it but live it, will help you thrive in the land of ambiguity in consumer innovation. As a leader, help your colleagues and direct reports to understand the importance of failure and how failing can feed back into the system focused on consumer-innovation. Lead by example, share where you have failed/learned and encourage others to do the same.

CHAPTER 13

It's Not About You!
Part One: Leadership
Principles to Live By

I am constantly reminded of the unrivaled value of strong leadership and mentorship, and their power to enact positive change. Over the past 20+ years, I have had the honor to lead all types of people, groups, and organizations. Some have been great, and some, well you know, not so great. But, there is one principle I have learned as a leader: It's not about me. It's about those who I lead.

Now let me be perfectly honest, I am not an expert at this. I still am challenged weekly and daily to walk the talk. Sometimes, I do really well, and sometimes, not so well. I have had several conversations over the past several weeks where this fact has resonated with me more than ever. Tom Peters states, "Leaders do not create followers, they create more leaders."

I have evolved professionally and personally as a mentee because of one of the greatest leaders in my life. I have watched this leader constantly challenge people to go beyond what they thought was possible. In fact, I am one of those people. This leader challenged me to take a risk, and I did. I have never looked back. Not only did he create another leader, but he created a follower and disciple of the principle; it's not about me.

As this leader was mentoring one of our colleagues, he said, "Think about what is possible, but then go do the impossible." He then asked the colleague, "If you could create your dream job, what would it be?" He also asked, "What do you really want to do?"

These are the same questions this leader asked me years ago, and ones he still asks of me today. I am constantly challenged to grow beyond what I think is possible and evolve into someone greater. My hope is that when I move on from this life, people will look at me as one who created opportunities, challenged people, and cultivated leaders.

This leader has also taught me to let go and allow others to do their jobs. I may not always agree with how the job is done — and therein lies one of my greatest challenges — to remember that it's not about me, but about them.

What does this all this mean? Jack Welch put it best when he said, "The day you become a leader, it becomes about them. Your job is to walk around with a can of water in one hand and a can of fertilizer in the other hand. Think of your team as seeds and try to build a garden."

In Brent Gleeson's *Forbes* article, "5 Steps for Leading Through Adaptive Change," the steps are basic:

1. **Give direction** – Communication is crucial and critical for a leader. We can never over-communicate to our teams and leaders.

2. **Provide protection** – Be the one willing to take the bullet. Protect others not only from internal politics but also from external.

3. **Clarify roles** – Provide direction and guidance each step of the way as roles are being transformed.

4. **Manage conflict** – Keep conflict away from colleagues and teams. It is your job to protect. (Remember, step two).

5. **Shape the norms** – It is your job to steer the ship, but not your job to do it by yourself. Bring the team along. Help them see the future and the new norm. They will follow.

What I Will Do with It ...

Jack Welch stated, *"The day you become a leader, your job is to take people who are already great and make them unbelievable."*

💡 A NOTE FROM STEVE

From years of working with executives on their development, the journey of becoming a leader never ends. Having worked with several amazing CEOs, they had a thirst for learning and improving their leadership capabilities. They were focused on building capabilities to help them lead their organizations into the future. Their "leadership by example" was visible to not only their direct reports but also to the entire organization.

Become a lifelong student of leadership. It is not about you. Through reflection, feedback, and self-awareness, you can pinpoint areas that are critical to leading in the future. You can help yourself and your people go from great to unbelievable.

I will continue to keep this thought in the front of my mind as I work with organizations to build their consumer-innovation practices. I will continue to coach my leaders around the fact that *"It's not about you, or even us. It is about them!"*

What You Can Do ...

Knowing that it is not about you, how will your leadership focus change? When you think about your role as a leader creating new leaders, how does that shift your mindset and the tactics you will use to create the next generation of leaders? Become a student of leadership. Find mentors both within your organization and externally. Study other industries, particularly the service industry, as those at the top are incredibly tuned in to the consumer and can help you transform your organization.

CHAPTER 14

It's Not About You!
Part Two: Leadership
Principles to Live By

I was introduced to the podcast "Five Leadership Questions" hosted by Todd Adkins and Barnabas Piper, presented by Lifeway Leadership. In every podcast, they ask their guests to answer the same five questions that are intended to inspire leaders, and then they share those insights and learning from other great leaders. Here are those five questions and my responses. I will revisit and change these over time; however, the important part is to spend some time to answer them for yourself. Maybe my responses will spark your thought process.

> Who are you learning from?

> What is the main point of emphasis for your leadership team (or self) right now?

> What obstacles are you currently facing in leadership, either in your organization or personally?

> What does leadership in your home look like?

> What would you tell your 20-year-old self about preparing to lead?

» **Who are You Learning From?**

I have focused on my ability to not only lead but to focus on what's next for me. *Pivot*, by Jenny Blake, has challenged me to not only think a bit differently but to also focus on me and what I want as a person.

» **What is the Main Point of Emphasis for Your Leadership Team (or Self) Right Now?**

I have had several conversations around the following questions: What's next for me? What is the next step in my career? Most importantly, I want my work to make me happy. So, the main point of emphasis for my leadership team and for myself is not to get into the weeds with our teams but to stay in front and lead. It is also to keep the leadership focus on them. Remember, it's not about me, but about them. Spend time with your team members, listen to them and help guide them on the path that is best for them.

» **What Obstacles are You Currently Facing in Leadership, Either in Your Organization or Personally?**

With the relaunch of The Nason Group, the biggest challenge facing my leadership while we are in bootstrap mode is leading in a start-up capacity, which is significantly different than being in an established corporation. What that means is that my focus is almost 100 percent on opening new doors and business opportunities while trusting the rest of the team is focused on everything from strategy to operations. Because we are moving fast, I need to slow down at times to ensure that we are all on the same page even though we might all be in different parts of the country.

» **What Does Leadership in Your Home Look Like?**

I believe leadership in my home looks like strength, protector,

♀ A NOTE FROM STEVE

These are fabulous questions to consider throughout your career. They are simple, help provide clarity and focus, and help you reflect to consider implications both individually and organizationally.

Imagine if leaders had this conversation several times per year? What impact would that have and more importantly, what behaviors would shift because of these questions? Would a discussion on obstacles at the most senior levels spur collaboration and insights on how to overcome those obstacles? Would a CEO sharing the advice they would tell their 20-year-old self inspire others to lead and to better know themselves?

provider, friend, parent, and lover. What does this mean? Not everyone who reads this blog is spiritual or religious, but I have to go back to the heart of leadership for me. God called us as men to be the covering for our families. He called me to be the protector, strength, provider, friend, parent, and lover. Now, by no means do I always get this right. You can ask my wife. But, I try every day to do this. I try to be the man I am called to be. The friend I am to be. The husband I am to be. The father I am to be. The leader I am to be.

» **What Would You Tell Your 20-Year-Old Self About Preparing to Lead?**

I would tell my 20-year-old self to run! No, not really. I would tell that young man always to stay true to who you are. Do not become something or someone others want you to be. Just. Be. You. For example, I have found starting up my company allows me to run as fast as I can, with those I want to run with, for as long as I want to run because it is mine. It has taken me many years and four professions to figure out where I am the fastest. I now find myself the happiest I have been in my career and where I feel the most authentic. The second most important piece of advice I would give is to always to put others first. Remember, you would not be a leader and where you are were it not for others.

Always listen! Always be there for -the people you lead! Always be true to yourself!

What I Will Do with It ...

I will continue to ask myself these critical questions to ensure I am being true to my mission, myself, and my family.

What You Can Do ...

Write out your responses to the questions above. Share them with your mentor, your partner, and trusted advisors. Ask yourself if how you see yourself is how others see you. If the answer is no, ask yourself "so what?" What can you do about it? Then, put those actions in place. More importantly, have those you lead fill out their responses and engage in a discussion with each of them to see where you can provide support and eliminate barriers. Share your responses with your direct reports, let them know where you are at, and encourage them to share their responses amongst each other.

Why Do You Hire a Crazy Person with Passion? Innovation is Why!

"You Hire Crazy People!"

That is my answer when I am asked how I hire people for innovation. There is so much truth to that statement (please do not be offended if you work in Innovation), but there is a part of you that has to be a little crazy to do this work no matter what industry you are in. Recently, I sat  down with one of our team members, Brownrygg Woolls and shot this quick video. Scan the above code on your phone to watch the video. Enjoy! *(https://videopress.com/v/jdlGQkrX)*

In the video, I reference a blog post I wrote titled "A Hustler, Hacker, Storyteller, Singer and Artist Walk Into A Bar." In that blog, I shared about the team I worked with at the time. Although I work with a slightly different team today the principle is still the very same. There must be DIVERSITY & DIFFERENT THOUGHTS PROCESSES on your team to make it a success. I do not allow myself to hire or partner with anyone like me (that would be very scary anyways!)

 In that same session with Brownrygg, he asked another question, "As a young person, how do you prepare for this field?" Scan the code to the left to hear my response.

(https://videopress.com/v/qofg9ipC)

Passion, Passion, Passion!

Why Passion? Any person with passion will run till' they cannot run anymore. They will dig in until they find the answer. As a leader, I remember two team members who, on paper, did not look to be the right fit, but something about them resonated with me. I knew they were right for the job. And guess what? They were! Yes, I believe in a foundation of education with any career, but as I stated in that short video, "Do not read a resume! Read the person! Read their passion!"

> *"I'd rather lose myself in passion than lose my passion."*
>
> — **Jacques Mayol** —

 A NOTE FROM STEVE

Building diverse teams is incredibly important in the work we do. In order to open doors, people have to be able to relate to you and that can come in all different forms.

In addition, a CEO at a company I worked at some years ago talked about the large view of diversity, beyond what we typically think about. He stated that in addition to traditional thoughts on diversity, he wanted us to bring in people to the organization who thought differently, were trained differently, and who came from different parts of the world.

It made sense. You don't want to hire all of your engineers from the same engineering school. You don't want to only hire people in your backyard. You also don't want to hire people who don't push back. Pride has to take a back seat. Creating a diverse environment takes the right mindset and leadership because it requires a constant focus and being uncomfortable with the current state. Find the passionate ones, they can be taught.

So, here is my challenge to you today as a leader or team member in the world of innovation: Surround yourself with diversity. Make sure you bring in skill sets that you do not have yourself. But most importantly, build a team filled with passion, and you can conquer anything! Go kick some ass today!

CHAPTER 15

Conquering Your Fear by Facing It!
Part Three: Leadership
Principles to Live By

When I first stepped into a leadership role, I never anticipated how often I would be expected to step outside my comfort zone and face my fears. Through the years, the one key lesson I've learned is if you do not face the fear — whatever it is — you will go right back around that mountain until you do. That leads me to a personal story and lesson I want to share with you.

I had the amazing opportunity to travel to Sydney, Australia to meet with colleagues on our team. The city was truly amazing and inspiring to me. As I am in the process of taking better care of myself, I choose to run three different days in three different areas of the city. WOW! Truly beautiful.

One evening, I rode a ferry through the Sydney Harbor and took a beautiful picture. It was in Sydney that I was presented with an opportunity to face one of my biggest fears personally; the fear of heights. (I will share more on that in just a bit).

On my way to Sydney, I had just read an article in *Harvard Business Review* titled, "If You're Not Outside Your Comfort Zone, You Won't Learn Anything." In this article, HBR presented three basic truths: be honest with yourself, make the behavior your own, and take the plunge. Three simple truths, but not always three simple things to do.

This gets me back to my story. When you are in Sydney you can avail yourself of what is known as the BridgeClimb Sydney. In this experience, you have the amazing opportunity to climb 1,332 steps and 440 feet above the water to reach the summit of the bridge. Now, for someone who has a fear of heights, doesn't this sound exciting? There was no way I was going to do this. The trouble is I had just read the article about being honest with myself, making the behavior my own, and taking the plunge. I thought to myself, I will call my wife, and she will talk me out of it. NOPE! She told me I should do it. So, for the

 next 24 hours, I contemplated and tried to talk myself out of it, but I just couldn't do it. I knew I had to face this fear or I was going to have to go around this mountain again. So, I DID IT! Scan the code to the left on your phone to watch the experience on video.

(https://videopress.com/v/9Xk6KgFW)

I have to say that it was one of the most rewarding experiences in my life, but also scary at times. So, what does this have to do with leadership? EVERYTHING!

Later that afternoon when I got back to my room, I sat down at my computer to answer some e-mails and a blog post titled, "Success Isn't Comfortable," came across my e-mail. I just had to laugh. They gave three principles for leaders to remember in the blog post.

» **First, leaders who learn to stretch their comfort levels and**

ask tough questions make better leaders and innovators.

» **Second, being uncomfortable and trying new things makes people more mentally flexible and creative.**

» **Last, accepting uncertainty, ambiguity, and change creates a comfort level with the unknown — an educated fearlessness today's leaders require.**

So, as a leader, there are days it may be rough, even tough and you may feel as if you just don't want to do it anymore, but you must. We

💡 A NOTE FROM STEVE

Working with and getting to know your consumers can drive significant fear and anxiety for some colleagues. Some people are introverts and asking them to stretch their comfort zone can actually take them into their "terror" zone. In those cases, we have to make it easy for people to interact with consumers.

One way we help people conquer their fear in speaking with consumers is a feet-on-the-street activity. During this activity, we have members of our teams go on the street after brainstorming questions, typically about a topic that is generated from a "How Might We ... " question. For example, "How might we improve the health of our members without transportation?" Participants go out in pairs or groups of three to solicit feedback from people on the street, everyday consumers.

(continued on following page)

(continued from previous page)

The purpose for this activity is not related to the answers we receive. It is meant to take participants through an experience where they have a good opportunity to experiment, fail, refine, and go back into the cycle, learning through each interaction with the consumer.

We focus intentionally on not providing too much feedback during brainstorming because consumer responses will quickly tell you if a) your questions make sense and b) you are gathering the types of insights that will help you respond to the question at hand. This model also helps the introverts who can observe and process differently the information (verbal and non-verbal) as we go into the debriefs and it is incredibly valuable. These insights are then used as part of any project efforts we have going on.

must be willing to stretch out of the comfort zones and be honest with ourselves and accept that we may not always have all the answers or the skills to get everything done. Being uncomfortable isn't fun, but as leaders, we do learn from it. I have not always wanted to take the plunge and do things outside my comfort zone, but in the end, 99 percent of the time I am glad that I did.

What I Will Do with It ...

I'm going to continue to be honest with myself and challenge myself by getting out of my comfort zone. I will continue to think about my leadership and more importantly, ACT on those things that I need to shore up. I will also continue to develop those who report to me and encourage them to step out of their comfort zones and take risks. In addition, I'll look for opportunities to coach those in other organizations and the community, to make a real difference. I will put myself out there for others.

What You Can Do ...

Have that moment of clarity and get real with yourself and how you lead yourself and others.

My challenge to you as a leader is:

> What are you going to do to get out of your comfort zone and take the plunge?

> How are you going to stretch beyond your current comfort level and ask yourself the tough questions?

> How will you challenge your leaders and those who report to you to also feel safe enough to stretch beyond their comfort zone and step into the unknown?

Silos: The Trees are Your Solution

For many leaders, while they understand their organization is siloed and this is stagnating their growth, finding direction can often feel like one is deep in the forest — unable to see through the trees.

But herein lies the magic. The trees are often where the solutions stand. You already know "your trees" — those key stakeholders within your organization who will champion, disrupt and cultivate dynamic open collaboration and empowered decision-making necessary for culture shifts and sustained organizational growth across all business units. Many trees: one forest. Many voices: endless potential!

> ### 💡 A NOTE FROM STEVE
>
> One group of "disruptors" readily available are your team members. If you are a leader, you would be surprised at how willing a colleague is to get out of their day-to-day work to try something new! They just need, and I hate this word, the "permission" space to step outside. As you develop the mindset that you don't have to ask for permission, you'll begin to build a culture of disruptors and collaborators, focused on solving problems for the consumer.

Over 25 years ago, Jack Welch championed what was then a groundbreaking concept — working across organizational boundaries and disrupting operational "norms." Welch felt that by designing shorter decision cycles, increasing employee engagement, and building a strong network of collaboration, companies could experience greater success. His theory became the GE Work-Out process, and it centered around creating a "boundary-less organization."

His idea was — and remains — genius. Provide the organization with a forum in which to collaborate, and problem solve — bringing key stakeholders together to share their skills, expertise, experiences, and insights. Use your internal talent. Innovate, inspire and collaborate: all in real time with the people invested in the success of an organization!

Decades later, far too many organizations still struggle from within their legacy-driven organizational structures. As Ron Ashkenas wrote in his 2015 *Harvard Business Review* Article "Still Works":

"Fast forward to today, and we live in a different world. Our communications technologies have dramatically improved. Welch's 'boundary-less organization' should seemingly be the de facto reality for most companies. To the contrary, however, many organizations still have hierarchical, siloed, and fragmented processes and cultures. In fact, having to cope with a fast-changing global economy has led many companies to create even more complex matrix organizations, where it's actually harder to get the right people together for fast decision-making."

In the book *Designing Your Life* by Bill Burnett and Dave Evans, the authors lay out five mindsets for us as individuals to use, but they are also key for organizations in helping break-down silos and include Curiosity — to be curious, Bias to Action — try stuff, Reframing — take problems and reframe them, Awareness — know it is a process, and Radical collaboration — ask and seek out help as needed.

"Silos have no place in our lives, let alone as an operational foundation of any business or corporation!"

— Shawn Nason —

Here is what Bill says about Radical Collaboration:

"This is perhaps the most important design thinking mindset in Life Design. The best designers know that great design requires radical collaboration. You are not (and should not be) alone. An artist can create a masterpiece holed-up in a cabin in the woods but a designer cannot create the next global, behavior changing piece of hardware solo. Your life is more like a great design than a piece of art. It is a collaborative process. Many of the best ideas will come from other

people, you just need to ask. Essentially, Life Design, like all design, is a team sport."

The sooner you build your Life Design team, the better. Engage the people you love and admire to work together, to design better lives individually — and as a community.

What I Will Do with It ...

I will continue to bring the five mindsets to life in everything I do. And when I fail, I will get back up and start over again. I'll break down silos and continue to build collaborative co-creating organizations that focus on consumer innovation. I'll build teams that engage across the organization and show others how to know the consumer and use those insights to innovate, and then I'll do it all over again — relentlessly focusing on the solutions in the trees.

What You Can Do ...

My challenge to you today is this: BREAK DOWN THE SILOS, both in your life and in your business! Go to the trees; take your team with you, and change the mindset of the organization to enable consumer-centered innovation to occur!

Together, Moving Mountains!

In a previous Chief Innovation role, I had the pleasure, along with several esteemed colleagues, to host a PitchFest. The PitchFest included 10 dynamic entrepreneurs who were given four minutes to share their most innovative ideas around transforming health and well-being. Each of the pitches was assessed by a panel of judges. What transpired far exceeded our expectations. At the end of the four hours, we had been introduced to 10 passionate, innovative,

💡 A NOTE FROM STEVE

I believe that innovation comes from key relationships. Too often, we decide that we can create or build it better than [insert name of any organization] instead of looking externally. This is a logical fallacy.

In the example of our inaugural PitchFest Shawn mentioned, we were able to identify a partner that already had a commercialized product available that could integrate into our existing offerings. It would have taken us months, possibly years to develop the technology, processes, etc.; however, moving mountains means sometimes you have to hire a bulldozer driver to plow down the barriers that stand in your way.

thought-provoking ideas, all addressing healthcare challenges from heart to toe — literally.

Each company was given three key tenants for their presentations: Know me. Surprise Me. Make It Easy. The ultimate goal for PitchFest was to learn who they were, the focus of their work, and their transformative solutions. Next, the judging panel looked for the fresh, innovative, and unexpected ideas and solutions to some of the biggest issues in healthcare. The winning solution needed to be easy to implement and to be purpose driven — allowing for a high probability of consumer engagement. Lastly, the solutions had to be comprehensive, and value-driven, adequately addressing the problem they presented — across the enterprise, provider, and patient platforms.

It was an enlightening four hours of passionate delivery by companies from all over the US and Finland. This supercharged event also attracted a collection of active community influencers across the local innovation, incubator and accelerator landscape.

As a sum, the presentations addressed not only the physical challenges of the healthcare consumer but their emotional and mental connectivity to their well-being journey. In the end, the sweet spot for transformational change lies in successfully connecting the healthcare consumer to their well-being journey and providing the enterprise for providers, payors, and investors with cost-effective results.

The ultimate winner of the PitchFest has made their focus diabetes medication and treatment management. The problem they specifically address is the lack of effective monitoring of both glucose and behavior management in patients — resulting in higher costs for both the enterprise, provider and patient. Through their solution, patient data is aggregated and used to predict a patient's glucose profile, allowing healthcare providers to drive blood glucose levels into the target through stronger medication management and behavior modifications. This solution offers health systems a path to delivering both quality and cost-effective treatment plans. By saying YES! to the concept of PitchFest and to this organization, we formed a partnership that benefited both of our organizations in bringing new technology to the fight against diabetes in this country.

I believe firmly in the value of partnering with the healthcare community, building relationships with entrepreneurs, and looking for opportunities to collaborate and co-create. At the end of the day, cultivating new relationships within the healthcare startup space is critical to growth. Using forums like PitchFest is proof that together, as visionaries focused on innovating the health and well-being space, we can move mountains!

What I Will Do with It ...

I will continue to say YES! to powerful opportunities to collaborate and co-create with innovative organizations. I will say YES! to being on PitchFest panels and supporting innovators and entrepreneurs. I will look to create forums where co-creation and collaboration can happen and that others are made more aware of the opportunities they may have overlooked while highlighting amazing entrepreneurs and innovators.

What You Can Do ...

Run your own PitchFest or similar event to increase collaboration and opportunities to co-create and collaborate on solutions for your consumers and those of your potential partners. It is not a significant investment; however, it provides significant returns. Sponsoring something like a PitchFest allows you to sponsor and be an organization that "gets innovation" and that invests in partnerships. The outcome you can expect at one end of the spectrum is to learn and begin to be an investor in innovation as well as a thought leader. On the other end of the spectrum is a full-blown partnership where each organization can leverage resources, consumers, etc., to fulfill aspects of each other's missions.

SECTION 3

The Power of YES! in Innovation ... Know Me, Surprise Me, Make it Easy

Why would we need an introduction to the consumer? Because no matter how many times we try to explain it's not about you, it's about the consumer. The consumer gets left out of the consumer-centered innovation process. Ironic, isn't it?

Oftentimes, we are brought in exactly for this reason: to help organizations understand and hear their customers and the consumer. We will bring them in to help collaborate and co-create side-by-side with organizations. We help organizations reach out to consumers to gain feedback and insights in how to provide better services and products. In addition to bringing in consumers and customers, we also share three key values to help guide our partners through the consumer-centered innovation process.

We help organizations bring to life their customers and consumers through our consumer principles and values: Know Me, Surprise Me, and Make It Easy, in our personal life as well as our work with partners. The values are so critical to supporting The Power of

YES! in Innovation and leading consumer-centered change that it required us to create a separate section to help you understand how they work together.

We not only provide an overview of these values, but we will also share how we have implemented these values and incorporated the values into the consumer-centered design work we have done at several organizations. The values were even used as a measurement for our success!

Why the values? It goes back to the first section of *The Power of YES! in Innovation,* when we discussed creating a consumer-centered innovation mindset. Using the values accelerates the organization's transition from a transactional organization to a consumer-focused innovation organization. The values are our "secret sauce" that have helped us catapult ahead of the pack.

Let's explore the principles, our values: Know Me, Surprise Me, and Make It Easy, starting from the perspective of the consumer, and in particular, with empathy.

💡 A NOTE FROM STEVE

Please steal any and/or all of the values Shawn discusses.
You have our permission. Having been immersed in these
values and other similar values at other organizations, there
is nothing more freeing than having values as guide posts
to think about everything I/we do from the perspective
of the consumer.

Know Me, Surprise Me, and Make It Easy enables the organization as well as me personally, to understand the "why"
of how we individually and collectively exist in addition to
providing a product or service. When you are able to connect
with and live these values, your mindset will change. What
you say yes to will have real and substantial impact on
your customers.

We have used these values at several stops along our journey
with the consumer. Yes, they do help shape the mindset. Yes,
the values help colleagues determine their priories as well as
the organization's priorities.

These values form the backdrop and our focus, so we need
committed colleagues to call bullshit, even with leadership.
Once the organization gets to the place where decisions
are made — both in line with your business model and the
values — it is pure CCI nirvana.

CHAPTER 16

Tap into Your Talent:
The Power of Empathy!

My team and I met with a healthcare organization to discuss transformative change around their consumer experience practices. Their CEO handpicked the attendees, and they represented all aspects of the company. Each one, in their own unique and specific way, held responsibility for consumer and employee experience. It was this CEO's hope that by bringing everyone to the table at once, collaboratively, they would begin to understand where they are as opposed to where they should be as an organization.

We met for three half days and worked through unique, thoughtful experiences designed to open eyes and hearts around what it truly means to meet the consumer "where they are" — what does that look like, feel like and how do we measure up?

At times, you could hear a pin drop as they watched short videos around empathy-driven, consumer-focused care delivery. There were inspiring moments of revelation when they connected the dots between what they do now and what they need to be doing to improve their consumer's experience.

For myself and my team, witnessing this connection can only be described as INSPIRING. I believe that all employees are committed to being the best they can be. Often, and especially in the healthcare industry, people consider their work a "calling." With this calling comes strong passion and a focus on making a difference. Herein lies the sweet spot — a gold mine of opportunity for an organization.

💡 A NOTE FROM STEVE

I like to call this the "scare the hell out of people" conversation. Actually, a better term would be more along the lines of "let's get real." As Shawn states, so many of us get caught up in accomplishing our day-to-day, that we forget about our customers and that's sad.

It is sad because our customers (current and future) can provide great insights into what really motivates them and makes them want to use what we offer. It goes beyond recommending us to a family member or friend; it means that together, we have formed a connection.

Take some of the best currently at knowing their customers — Disney, Marriott International, and Delta to name a few. Their focus today is on incremental or core innovation, making the experience of their customers even one percent better supports their brand, retention, and attracting new customers. What's common amongst all of these organizations and why are they successful?

They. Know. Their. Customer.

Unfortunately, over time, business units within well-meaning organizations can become siloed. They unconsciously disconnect from one another in the process of achieving their department-specific goals of creating, managing and delivering the customer experience. The fallout is that the customer experience becomes lost or convoluted as the focus shifts more to meeting a goal rather than meeting the customer where they are. In addition, employees can begin to lose sight of purposeful, meaningful engagement with their work.

As part of the events, we met with key stakeholders identified by the CEO. This was when we recognized where the exciting potential for transformation lies. This company holds a wealth of passionate visionaries, extraordinary talent, and invaluable experience in its people. Some have been with the organization for decades. Some are new. They all offered candid and thoughtful insights into the barriers, possibilities, and strategies they believe are necessary to enact a successful organizational pivot. More importantly, they all are ready to take the next step toward innovating and transforming their customer's experience — both internally and externally. What is needed from this point is where a great many companies fall silent.

What I Will Do with It ...

I will continue to say YES! to walking into the unknown with my partners to help them develop consumer-focused strategies. I will share thoughts with executives around the country to influence and encourage them to really get to know their consumers. I will keep doing what I do — just at scale — through books like this and future books that will go more deeply into the "how-to" aspect of building organizations that are consumer-innovation focused.

What You Can Do ...

Explore opportunities to speak with people who are focused on the consumer or who would like to focus on the consumer. Walk over to the customer support area, the grievances area, and follow your company on Facebook, Twitter, Instagram, LinkedIn, Snapchat, etc. Use the insights you gather from hearing and listening to the consumer as part of your day-to-day work. Social media enables the consumer to be brutally honest and provides you with insights that you may have never been able to see previously.

CHAPTER 17

How EMPATHY and DESIGN THINKING Wrecked My Life!

Over the past several years, I have been on a personal journey to decide what I want to be when I grow up. My wife, Carla, would say, "He still doesn't know, because he will never grow up." What I never realized on this road of discovery was how much developing one trait in my life would impact who I am.

EMPATHY

Empathy is the ability to share and understand the feelings of others.

Now, let me say this, I am no expert at it, and I am still on this journey, but empathy should be at the core of each one of us. I spent several years of my life as a pastor. A great deal of my time was dedicated to understanding the places, feelings, and situations people were going through.

It WRECKED me.

Why did it wreck me? Those experiences went to my soul.

I was transformed daily by:

> The mother who did not know how to deal with her teenager, because I became that struggling parent trying to connect to her teenager. It was so frustrating.

> The wife trying to connect with her husband, but who felt hopeless and defeated, because I became that spouse as I tried to understand her point of view. It was so heartbreaking.

> The child who just wished his parents would understand him, because I became that child and I understood just how painful and lonely it was to feel misunderstood, alone, and unloved. It was agonizing.

> The widower who lost his best friend after 50 years of marriage, because I became that husband and could understand the size of the hole in his heart. It was devastating.

Yes, these experiences were frustrating, heartbreaking, agonizing, and devastating, and they didn't HAPPEN TO ME! But, I could empathize. I could feel the peoples' heartache and pain. I walked with them. Though I was by no means suffering the way they were; I was nevertheless able to feel deeply for them.

Empathizing is not easy. It should wreck you! It should shake you to the core. And it has done just that to me — to my life. I am so grateful for the people I have met, who have shared their struggles because I have learned so much from them. It has strengthened and enlightened my entire life and it started with my own mother.

My mother had a heart of gold and would give the very shirt off her back, but also the shirt off my back, my brother's back, and my dad's back. Though she used to tell us, "We will not give a handout, but a helping hand." (I can attest, she gave more than a hand)! How I miss so much of that wisdom today. My mother gave her life helping

💡 A NOTE FROM STEVE

At some point during our workshops, sprints, etc., you will cry! Is it a guarantee? No. But it has happened every time we've worked with our partners in helping them get to know their customers.

We brought in a consumer who liked to call herself Foxy Brown. Ms. Brown had a medical condition; however, because she was a caregiver for one of her very ill family members and the matriarch of the family, she did not take care of herself. When Ms. Brown told her story, many of us cried. We could feel the struggle she faced every single day.

We cried again later that day when the CEO of the organization we were working with came down to speak with Ms. Brown. The CEO had been in meetings all day; however, word got out that one of their consumers had really touched the group that she was working with on creating various prototypes. The CEO had a fabulous conversation with Ms. Brown. The last question he asked her was for permission to give her a hug to thank her for sharing her story and helping his organization make a difference not only for her but for others in the future. We all felt it and very few of us could hold back the tears of joy that told us we were going to make a difference not only for Ms. Brown but for so many other people.

You will be wrecked in the most magnificent way.

others and building them up to succeed. Through her example
of selflessness and generosity, I have learned how to be a leader,
a father, and a friend.

It WRECKED me.

How? Today as I walk in the mall, the grocery store, the mall on
our campus, or just in the office, I stop and think about what might
that person be going through today that I have never experienced.
Through a work project, I spent several months in the wonderful
state of Mississippi to understand how poverty affects health, and
I learned what it was like to really be hungry and to be unable to meet
one's basic needs. I learned EMPATHY in such a real and raw way.

I watch my wife daily not only love our seven-year-old daughter,
but also our newborn son. I have never seen empathy seep out of
the pores of one human being like I see it come out of hers. She did
not give birth to these children, but she has the ability to share and
understand their feelings. She can communicate and love them from
the depths of her being.

It WRECKED me.

As a mother, she has taught me to be a better father. She has taught
me to set aside my wants and desires. Daily, I see her set her wants
and desires aside to make sure our kids' needs and wants are met.
Some days, I know it is tough, but she does it with a smile on her face
(most of the time.) She has taught me not to be so serious, but to just
love them and have the time of our lives watching them grow-up.

What does all of this have to do with DESIGN THINKING?

Everything.

Design thinking teaches you to learn how to empathize. First, by putting yourself in someone else's shoes, experiences, trials, or even successes. I have spent the last several years working with the Goliaths of the world to help move the needle when it comes to empathy. From a patient's experience in the doctor's office to the guest's experience when they walk into your park — the consumer, the guest, the customer, the student (whatever you want to call them or should call them in your respective industry) are always (and should always) be FIRST!

I get the honor every day to work with a team and community that not only believes and practices this, but it is at the core of who they are. They love to understand what the student, the patient, the member, the colleagues, etc., is going through. They love to understand the problem the business or team we are working with is facing. They let this pour out of everything they do, and I get to watch it, live it, and love it!

So, how did empathy and design-thinking wreck my life? By one simple thing, it *is* my life! It *is* who I have become. It *is* who I will forever be. As I stated earlier, I am not perfect, and I do not always do it right. But as a leader, a husband, a father, and a friend, I try to remember what everyone is going through or facing that day — and it wrecks me — in the best possible way.

To all of you I say, thank you for sharing your life with me. I am a better person because of each of you!

What I Will Do with It ...

I will keep trying on different shoes and better understand and empathize with consumers across the globe.

What You Can Do ...

Find opportunities to empathize with consumers. Sometimes, it is easier to start with your inner circle, your family, co-workers and/or friends. Ask them about their experiences as a consumer. Spend time doing "elevator interviews" if you happen to have an office with an elevator, or lunchtime interviews while waiting in line for lunch with colleagues. Take the bold step of asking a question ... listening, and then following up with another question. Most importantly, listen and try on that other person's shoes.

CHAPTER 18

Seeing with Eyes, Listening with Ears, and Feeling with the Heart!

I have had the privilege to travel multiple times to the United Arab Emirates (UAE) region, specifically Dubai. What is a Chief Innovation/Transformation Officer doing in Dubai?"

I was asked to speak at one of the leading healthcare investment conferences in the Gulf Cooperation Council (GCC) and UAE region. I was honored to share the platform with such leaders as H.E. Dr. Amin Hussain Al Amiri, the Assistant Undersecretary of Public Health Policy & Licensing for the Ministry of Health in the UAE, as well as Dr. Raza Siddiqui, Group CEO of the Arabian Healthcare Group, and finally, with Gregory Schaffer, CEO, Tawam Hospital, Johns Hopkins Medicine International.

So, what does this trip have to do with empathy?

Everything.

Everything I have been taught to believe about this area of the world has been challenged. In the short time that I have been in Dubai, I have fallen in love with this beautiful region and most of all, the beautiful people. Dubai represents more than 200+ nationalities, multiple religious beliefs, and all walks of life. I visited the local market, ate in local restaurants, and walked on one of the most beautiful beaches in the world.

As an Innovation Executive, I spend most of my time working with teams, leaders, and innovation seekers using human-centered design and the principles of design thinking. I had to step back and use those principles. I spent several days talking to other participants

💡 A NOTE FROM STEVE

It is so important to look outside your environment to gain perspective on the consumer. Whether it be out of industry, or looking at a problem from the perspective of another part of the world, opening up your eyes to what's beyond your walls is critical.

As we work with our partners, we often push them hard to look beyond their walls. Looking internally is what's caused them to lose touch with their customers. Looking externally allows them to see, think, and feel differently about their customers. Looking beyond the walls of your own organization sparks ideas and questions.

And you don't necessarily have to travel to experience aspects of this viewpoint. Through so many technology capabilities and social networking platforms (e.g. Twitter and LinkedIn), it's easy to reach out to someone to seek out incredible insights. It takes stepping out of your comfort zone and letting your desire to empathize with your customers compel you to go beyond your walls.

about empathy and displacing judgment. I have also shared the other important steps in the design thinking process, specifically how to ideate, prototype, and test.

Over several trips to Dubai, I have learned that the region's healthcare system needs these skills. The organizations are hungry for a higher quality of healthcare, a more patient-centered approach, and most of all, they are looking to move forward into the future. I shared consumer trends of 2020 and beyond, the budding trends in healthcare within the United States, and our thought leadership around consumer-centered innovation!

What I Will Do with It ...

I will continue to explore consumer experiences outside my city, state, and country to build deeper insights and understanding of how various cultures approach similar challenges. Through this global perspective, I will share how this knowledge can impact my team and the organizations I work with and lead.

What You Can Do ...

So, my challenge to everyone who reads this is:

See with the eyes of others. Listen with the ears of others. Feel with the hearts of others.

You can get a much broader view of the consumer by looking outside of the United States — seek out that viewpoint. Generating consumer insights doesn't mean just from your customers but from consumers in general. What would it be like for you to create or extend products or services for those outside the current makeup of your customers?

How would you successfully engage those new consumers and tailor your product or service without ever speaking to them?

Know. Your. Consumer.

CHAPTER 19

Compassionate Leveraging of Your Consumer's Emotional Motivators

In 2016, three key consumer trends (communication platforms, wearable technologies, and socially responsible organizations) focused on the leveraging of human emotion and garnering an understanding of consumers' emotional motivators: seeing them as people first, and consumers second. This is, in our mind, one of the most significant touch points for an innovative forward-focused organization.

Organizations who want to build out a strong, viable stream of growth and profitability for the future, need to look beyond standard metrics around consumer satisfaction and brand awareness, and analyze the key emotional motivators driving current and potential customers. Understanding what motivates consumer loyalty allows for strategic and quantifiable measurement — aligning their motivations with the value it will or will not bring to your brand. Are you marketing to the right consumer and in a way that touches upon their emotional motivator? How do you find this out?

While brand value is cultivated by identifying consumer desire, developing an understanding of your client's unique emotional motivation is more science than art and coming up with quantifying results can be challenging. That said, quantifiable strategies are critical and are proving to be very effective across the brand board.

To assist organizations to understand and utilize the often unmined value that is part of a consumer's emotional motivation, Scott Magids, Alan Zorfas and Daniel Leemon spent eight years developing what they consider to be the standard lexicon of emotions. In the course of their research, they mined anthropological and social science research and spoke with numerous experts — ultimately assembling a list of 300 known emotional motivators.

♀ A NOTE FROM STEVE

The Maids, Zorfas and Leemon's finding that great advertising and consumer focus don't necessarily translate into emotional connection hit me to the core. Knowing we have so much data at our finger tips to segment our populations, social data to help us better understand behavior, and so much more data available to us is fantastic. And, all this data allows for your customer and the consumer to be overshadowed or even lost amongst the segmentations, models, numbers, etc. Consumers are not data points; we are real people!

So, how do you achieve that emotional connection? Three ways let us approach emotionally connecting with customers through our consumer values of know me, surprise me, and make it easy. These three values allow us to look at and humanize solutions — to connect at an emotional level.

In a recent article in the *Harvard Business Review*, "The New Science of Customer Emotions," the team stated, "At the most basic level, any company can begin a structured process of learning about its customers' emotional motivators and conducting experiments to leverage them, later scaling up from there. At the other end of the spectrum, firms can invest in deep research and big data analytics or engage consultancies with specific expertise."

In the following chart, you'll see a list of the 10 motivators that Magids, Zorfas, and Leemon found to be the most critical in defining an actual value for a consumer. It is an enlightening resource.

I am inspired by a desire to	Brands can leverage this motivator by helping customers:
Stand out from the crowd	Project a unique social identity; be seen as special
Have confidence in the future	Perceive the future as better than the past; have a positive mental picture of what's to come
Enjoy a sense of well-being	Feel that life measures up to expectations and that balance has been achieved; seek a stress-free state without conflicts or threats
Feel a sense of freedom	Act independently, without obligations or restrictions
Feel a sense of thrill	Experience visceral, overwhelming pleasure and excitement; participate in exciting, fun events
Feel a sense of belonging	Have an affiliation with people they relate to or aspire to be like; feel part of a group
Protect the environment	Sustain the belief that the environment is sacred; take action to improve their surroundings
Be the person I want to be	Fulfill a desire for ongoing self-improvement; live up to their ideal
Feel secure	Believe that what they have today will be there tomorrow; pursue goals and dreams without worry
Succeed in life	Feel that they lead meaningful lives; find worth that goes beyond financial or socioeconomic measures

Once you have conducted your research and have a clear or clearer understanding of who your consumer is at their core, it's time to work on the hard part. Figuring out the magic formula that will separate your brand from similar brands — consumer loyalty — is fickle and keeping them believing in you, is again, more science than art.

In a follow-up article to their earlier report in the *Harvard Business Review*, Magids, Zorfas, and Leemon asked: "What Separates the Best Customers from the Merely Satisfied?" They discovered, after further research involving hundreds of brands in dozens of industries, that when a consumer is emotionally connected to a brand, they are "anywhere from 25 percent to 100 percent more valuable in terms of revenue and profitability than those consumers who are "merely' satisfied with it." The article offered these four main points to consider:

> › Great advertising and consumer focus don't necessarily translate into emotional connection.

> › Just because a brand is ubiquitous doesn't mean it's making strong emotional connections.

> › You don't have to be an upscale brand to connect emotionally.

> › Variations within industries can be dramatic.

Consumers seek products and services to provide a sense of security, uniqueness, power, and accomplishment. If they are not emotionally connected to your brand, they are not going to remain loyal and will be looking for their next "emotional motivating" fix with another company. You don't have to be the biggest on the block, or the first, but you do have to be the most authentic. Between the lines in all the research is a fundamental truth: We all want to be treated as valuable to the companies we support. In this economy, as perhaps never before in the economic history of the US, consumers are demanding to be seen, heard, and communicated with in ways that make sense to them — demanding through their purchasing power, respect for their time, intelligence, and money. The trick is taking the science and humanizing its application.

Once you have a strategy in place and begin to gather your consumer's unique emotional motivators and have weighed their potential value — both in revenue and engagement through your organization — you are ready to disrupt, innovate and transform the way you engage, reward, and retain your most complicated and valuable asset: your consumer.

What I Will Do with It ...

I will continue to work with my organizations to help them understand the emotional motivators of their consumers and the implications of their products and services.

What You Can Do ...

Discover how to connect to your consumers on an emotional level by learning their stories, doing ethnographic research, interviewing them in their homes, etc.

CHAPTER 20

The Power of a Premium Consumer Experience

All of us have experienced it from time to time — the Power of a Premium Consumer Experience! Whether it is on the phone or in person, you leave the experience feeling special.

The Story ...

Recently, our team began working with one of our partners to lay the foundation for this type of premium experience for their members. Two of the foundational tools we use are ethnographic research and empathy mapping. During this process, we did live interviews, made phone calls, and created "How Might We" statements. Two of the test phone calls were to healthcare companies, and one to a service-based company.

Let me say this, two of those experiences were anything but premium, and one did not let us down at all. They provided fantastic service. Now I know, you want to know the names of those companies — but I am not going to reveal them now. With that said, you can probably guess which ones were which, but I will tell you, both of our calls within the healthcare industry were not only dis-satisfactory but overall, unhelpful. The one we had with the service industry went above and beyond to not only meet our needs but exceed them.

What We Learned ...

I have stated over and over again, that there is so much to learn from organizations that are service-based and built around the needs of the consumer. Recently, I read an article on the "Five Companies With Envy-Worthy Customer Experience." The companies are Zappos, Publix, Southwest Airlines, USAA, and Nordstrom. I have had personal experience with four of them, and they each focus on the consumer first and above anything else. I want to share a bit of my experience with Publix. For those of you who do not know Publix, they are a grocery store. I no longer live where there is a Publix, and miss it every day. When we travel back to where we can find one, we make it a point to shop there. Why? Because they lived by the three principles we live by here at The Nason Group.

They KNEW US, SURPRISED US, AND MADE IT EASY FOR US to shop there. Whether it is knowing our name or our tastes — they consistently meet our needs and make us feel like we are number one!

What We Can Do ...

The Power of a Premium Consumer Experience has no price tag. As The Nason Group works with partners, we cannot stress this enough. Our value proposition to organizations is that we MEET PEOPLE WHERE THEY ARE! Invest up front to meet your consumer where they are and it will not only bring loyalty but ultimately revenue and profits to your business. We will continue to live by this motto and encourage every one of our partners to do the same.

💡 A NOTE FROM STEVE

I think a key to any Premium Consumer Experience is understanding that we are not qualified to identify the experience. Deep empathy and knowledge of the consumer informs that premium experience.

Oftentimes, many smart people get into a room for months and design the experience, and roll it out. Wondering all along why consumers or customers didn't respond as expected. The answer always lies outside your walls and the walls of your organization. Too often, fear gets in the way of stepping into the unknown and causes us to focus internally.

Get. Out. Now.

What You Can Do ...

Take 30 minutes this week and spend time with your consumer. Ask them three simple questions.

> ❯ What do you like about our product or service?

> ❯ What is one thing you would change about our product or service?

> ❯ How can we get to know you better?

CHAPTER 21

Who the Hell are We Designing for? Healthcare: The Future Is Now!

I had the opportunity to spend three days with 70+ future forward movers and shakers in Austin, Texas. Our group, Innovation Learning Network, focused on becoming Architects of Better Futures & the Rites of Passage of the 21st Century: The 10-Year Landscape with The Institute for The Future. Then we looked at Discussing Design Without Losing Your Mind, Smarter Design for Smarter Decisions, and Caregiving 2031.

We also had our minds blown away when we discussed Future Vision from investment, retail, and culinary arts views. All these sessions were incredibly thought-provoking and challenging for me as both an innovator and learner. But, what I want to focus on is my experience on our Innovation Safari.

Imagine this! You are attending a conference with 70+ health-care leaders, and you break into groups of six to trek out into the city. Maybe we will go visit a hospital. Maybe a clinic in an unde-served area. It must be we are going to go visit a design studio in Austin. Nope!

We went to a restaurant. That's right a good ol` BBQ restaurant. The question I asked myself was, *How is this going to help me in the future when it comes to healthcare?* Let me tell you this; it was mind-blowing.

The BBQ establishment we went to visit was Rudy's — owned and operated by K&N Management based out of Austin. This was one of the most impactful afternoons I have ever had. Our team had the privilege to spend an hour with the general manager from the location we'd visited. He had been with the company for 18 years and worked his way up from a cashier in college, to a managing partner, his current position at that time. We spent an hour learning about PROCESSES, PROCESSES, PROCESSES.

So what?

K&N Management has been honored to win the coveted Malcolm Baldridge National Quality award. We learned that "The Love of Excellence" is what has caused this great success. Additionally, that afternoon we met with one of the executives who shared the company's journey with us. In this session, excellence was the theme. The key learning I walked away with was this; if you focus on one thing, and get everyone in the company focusing on it, you can move the needle!

That evening, I started thinking about how we could apply all of this to a system that lives in processes but is so many light-years behind. The next morning, as we listened to the discussion on Future Vision — it clicked.

Gary Hoover spoke to us about consumers, and he made one simple statement, "Whenever the consumer is involved, that's where innovation is!" Many organizational leaders talk about it, but very few practice it. Gary continued on to share the second nugget from that morning.

He stated, "To make a difference in healthcare, we need to study the great service organizations of the past and of today!"

💡 A NOTE FROM STEVE

Shawn and I make it a point to work with our partners and to look out of the industry at examples of innovation in the pursuit of redesigning Healthcare. Too often, we seek out those recognized in journals and we get the same information that everyone else has received through their benchmarking. We like to look in the corners at small and medium-sized businesses that are innovating.

In Shawn's case, visiting the BBQ joint was a HUGE spark in the work we do. While it might not seem obvious, we talk a lot about learning from others' processes and how they engage or interact with the consumer. The service industry is rich with examples across the spectrum from horrible to excellent. Just pull up Yelp! or Trip Advisor and read reviews — then go explore.

When you get to your destination, be "in" the experience as a consumer and when finished, ask to speak to a manager. Managers and those serving love to talk about your experience especially when it resembles excellence. And, even when it doesn't, you can learn a lot about what differentiates those that are excellent.

Well, I had done just that the day before. Service at its best.

I knew I had to apply both of those experiences to my day-to-day life to impact and change healthcare for the better. No longer will I bite off the whole system. We will pick one thing, and one thing only. Focus on that, and make a difference.

My teams will look at the past and learn from those before us, but we will also stride into the future with one thing in mind, the consumer — and only the consumer. Whether it is a member, patient, or provider — Focus on one thing and do it well!!!

So, who the hell are we designing for? YOU!

What I Will Do with It ...

I will continue to look at the past as well as the future, particularly the service industry. I will work with teams to relentlessly focus on one thing to drive excellence from the perspective of, and on behalf of the consumer.

What You Can Do ...

What organizations do you belong to that help you expand your knowledge of the consumer? What groups similar to ILN could you join to build your network and knowledge around consumer-innovation? What other industries might you look at outside of your own to draw parallels and learn from their consumers and strategies they have employed? You don't have to go far — start local and expand!

Also, what one thing could you focus on to become excellent?

CHAPTER 22

Who is the System Designed for? Consumerism: The Priority in Healthcare!

My life and career create experiences and innovations that focus on the consumer rather than the provider, patient, nurse, or vendor.

As Gary Hoover stated, *"To make a difference in healthcare we need to study the great service organizations of the past and of today!"* Gary was right! The following are several personal examples.

My wife and I had an opportunity to celebrate our wedding anniversary in Las Vegas. On our return trip, we had an incredible experience with a flight attendant. Carla My wife picks up the story.

[Carla] Just got off Delta flight 1075 from Las Vegas to Minneapolis. We were promptly greeted by our flight attendant, Vincent. Let me just tell you, that he should give a master class on proper customer service. He was so gracious and so accommodating as well as charming. If you are ever fortunate enough to be on one of his flights, consider yourself lucky. He's a wonderful asset to the Delta family!!!!!

That whole flight was dynamite for both of us! He made us feel like we were number one the entire flight while taking care of 14 other passengers. It was absolutely an amazing experience.

In our second example, my colleague one Saturday evening needed to visit the emergency room to have her foot looked at. When I read her post on Facebook I was mortified for her, and shocked that she was treated as she was — but the nugget in it all is the end of the story. I will share more on that after you read excerpts from her experience.

> *Last night, I finally reached out to my daughter to take me to a local Hospital ER. The pain in my foot had finally gnawed through my wall and I cracked. I was nauseous and experiencing chills.*
>
> *A lack of empathy from the front desk became clear from the moment my daughter struggled to help me into the wheelchair once inside the ER — as a nurse watched from behind the counter and never moved or offered to get help. I was hobbling in on one foot and clearly in need of some assistance. A short time later, I was wheeled back to be evaluated. That nurse was disengaged, unsympathetic and her heart elsewhere than in the moment with this pain ravaged, exhausted patient.*
>
> *Then, the tide turned. Once in the hands of the nursing staff, I experienced true empathy-driven care. Rich concern, detailed care and immediately at ease. The x-ray techs even wished me a belated birthday. The ER doctor was one of the kindest physicians I have come across in a long time. Factual, but with a warm and genuine bedside manner. In all things a pain baby, I was embarrassed to be of inconvenience to my daughter who had just worked 12 hours straight.*

My daughters both work in patient services in the ER for two different hospitals. Watching my daughter react to the initial care I received said a lot for how she views her responsibility to the patient. Interestingly, I found myself not wanting her to cause a stir — completely unlike me — and realized that as a patient, I just wanted to be cared for compassionately. How many times do patients just silently accept such blatant lack of compassion? More often than not I would say after my experience!

That final sentence was my gold nugget. This colleague is a confident, outspoken female, but she sat quietly and did not want to disturb the

---

💡 A NOTE FROM STEVE

Empathy is a cornerstone of design thinking as well as Consumer-Centered Innovation — the model we use to help partners know their customers or consumers. A good way to build empathy is to walk a day in the life of your customers and consumers.

In the case of Healthcare, this typically includes members or patients. However, there are many other layers of customers and consumers involved in providing Healthcare. To practice real empathy in healthcare, we need to broaden our perspectives and walk in the shoes of those additional customers and consumers, including physicians, pharmacists, nurses, etc.

Bottom line: you can never have enough empathy for all those involved in supporting the member or patient! Through empathy, you can be more precise with the opportunities and the important problems that must be solved.

system. She just wanted a compassionate experience. She wanted to be treated with dignity ... like a human! That's all! After I read that post, I knew I had to continue to work passionately toward top-notch experiences for all patients!

What I Will Do with It ...

The service industry has a lot to offer and inspire us in this space. So, let's study it, learn from it, and implement their methodologies around the consumer experience. I will invest more of my time in studying the service industry and identify conferences to attend, journals to subscribe to, etc.

What You Can Do ...

Will you join the cause? Will you share your consumer experience, especially those that delight you? Will you study other industries outside of your own and become a student of excellence in service?

CHAPTER 23

Meeting the Customer Where They Are – Customer Forums

With each turn of a new year, many organizations begin to review or employ updated customer experience strategies for their clients. Regardless of the type of customer your organization serves, some interesting and engaging trends are forecasted for the upcoming year. In an article for *Customer Think*, Richard Shapiro offers a list of his top 16 customer experience trends. We found four on his list to be of great interest and thought we would look at how these trends align with innovation and our goal to meet the customer where they are.

As you know, innovation of and by itself is a positive, yet disruptive process. To be truly innovative means that you are willing to open the door to ideas and concepts you might not have previously considered to be of value to your organization or customer. It also means in the process, there are ideas and approaches once successful that are now stale, that must be left on the table in pursuit of improving the customer experience.

The first customer experience trend we will look at is the expected increase in the customer's reliance on community forums to get information and to use in the instances of issue resolution. Customer forums, along with self-service, are tools that require creative and innovative models to work properly for both your organization and the client. Organizations must successfully drive their customers to the resource and then provide a robust and engaging interface, ensuring the overall experience exceeds the customer's expectation. For organizations to develop and implement high customer engagement, they must have a customer-centric strategy, and actively engage with the customer at all touchpoints in the customer experience.

At The Nason Group, we specialize in engaging the consumer and community in all steps within the process, from ideation to implementation. Whether it be a process or a product, the consumer and community are your organization's most valuable resource for success.

We have worked with a group of executives within the healthcare space on re-imagining how they will react with their consumer in a non-traditional manner within the industry. Although this journey with them has just begun, The Nason Group already sees favorable changes in both culture and attitudes taking place within the organization. Over the next six months, the successive steps will be for them to deploy this new strategy to their consumers.

The customer of today is tech-savvy and mobile. Organizations need to understand that the client wants to garner meaningful information from your organization at their convenience and any hour of the day. Businesses must provide their target audience with up-to-date, easy-to-access information regarding the services and products purchased, or perhaps those they intend to buy. Approach this trend with a goal of transparent access between you and your customer — answering their questions as quickly and directly as possible, and providing all necessary data up front. Today's customer

💡 A NOTE FROM STEVE

Trends are incredibly important indicators of the future. One mistake organizations make is going "all-in" by responding to trends without testing with their customers and consumers. Insights gathered will indicate directionally what nuances are important to your customers and that can make or break their experience.

The other thing is that we frequently discuss trends in working with the CEOs and their direct reports. Often, we find that organizations especially aren't tapped into consumer trends and rarely discuss those trends in the context of their business model. We work with senior leaders to interpret the potential implications to their business — leading the discussion on opportunities, investments, and threats.

If you aren't looking at trends — consumer, technology, etc., you can be sure that at least one of your competitors are and they are also determining where to focus to gain a competitive advantage.

is easily connected through the Internet to other customers and other customer experiences — good and bad. Rather than the old silo approach for managing information shared and controlling messaging, it is imperative that your customer forums are carefully planned, with open portals to every possible aspect of value to your customer. It is also key that you meet your customers where they are — providing them with individual attention, following up promptly on their concerns, garnering their opinions and being open to evolving your approach to ensure success for both you and the customer.

In this fast-paced digitally-driven world, staying aware of customer experience trends is vital. Successful businesses keep abreast of change and consistently innovate through listening, personally engaging with their clients, and staying out in front of their client's needs, driving a renewable, positive and enriched customer experience that benefits both the organization and the people it serves.

What I Will Do with It ...

I will continue to stay on top of industry trends so I can share the application of those trends with my current and future customers. When people hire me, they hire me for many reasons — including my knowledge of the trends that could impact their consumer strategies and competitiveness.

What You Can Do ...

Look at future consumer trends to determine what's potentially applicable to your environment. Knowing what's coming up can do one of two things: First, it should scare you if you aren't aware of the latest consumer trends because it means that you are already behind. These trends play both into your strategy, as well as your competitors. Second, knowing where the larger consumer trends are headed can provide insight as to where you should invest time, energy, and other resources — exploring how to tap into the trends from your own perspective.

CHAPTER 24

What a Toilet, a Car, and a Mouse Can Teach You!

Alan Ayers discusses how all of us have been "wronged" by bad consumer experiences in his post titled "The Injustice of Bad Customer Service." We all love to talk about them, post them on social media, and get our friends involved in the experience. Let me be honest here; I have been one of those people.

After many years of working for The Walt Disney Company, I have a very high expectation when it comes to customer service and consumer experience. My dear wife, Carla, hates when we go into a restaurant, and the experience starts to go bad.

She knows that there is something inside me that can't let it go. Maybe it is my years as a server, my years being around the restaurant business, or perhaps it comes down to plain common courtesy. I do not believe I ask for much, but I do expect to be treated like a human and a consumer that matters — whether it be in a restaurant, a store, with a doctor, or on airplane.

It comes back to the three basic principles I preach: Know Me, Surprise Me, and Make It Easy for Me!

So, what can we learn about consumer-centered experiences from a toilet? Or a car? Or even a mouse? Everything!

Let's start with the car!

Tesla disrupted an industry driven by traditional companies doing the same ol' thing. They built an experience where they KNOW who their consumer is and they create a flawless experience for them. This is the KNOW ME in the world of consumer-centered experiences.

A Toilet!

Andrew Griffiths in his blog post, "Japanese Toilets Taught Me a Lot About Customer Service," shared his experience of being in Japan and going to public toilets. He states, "I have never been in any toilet that isn't spotlessly clean, stocked with toilet paper, the soap dispensers are all full, and all of the hand dryers work."

What I see in his experience is the element of SURPRISE! Wouldn't it be wonderful if every restaurant, hotel, or store would pay that much attention to us as consumers to truly SURPRISE US in all our interactions?

A Mouse!

As I mentioned above, I spent many years working for the Walt Disney Company. In those years, although I was not a front of the house cast member, I learned a lot about how to MAKE IT EASY for our guests.

One of the great joys for me was to walk out into the park and witness a child seeing Mickey Mouse or Cinderella for the first time. It brought such joy to my day.

Disney is known all over the world for crafting magical experiences, along with meeting and exceeding their guests' expectations.

Therefore, today, my family and I still visit the park even without benefits or discounts.

In an article titled, "How Disney Creates Magical Experiences," Gregory Ciotti shares a story that explains how to MAKE IT EASY: "Many times, a guest will ask, 'What time does the 3:00 P.M. parade start?'" Well to us that may seem like a dumb question, but it is not. What that guest wants to know is, "What time will the parade come by here, where I am sitting or standing?" A Disney cast member could easily say, "It starts at 3:00 P.M..," but they are trained to say, "It

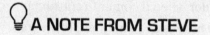
A NOTE FROM STEVE

I cannot emphasize enough the importance of consumer values! Steal ours or create your own; just ensure that you have them!

Why?

Consumer values enable your customer/consumer-facing team members to take ownership and solve problems.

Consumer values enable employees several layers away from interacting with the consumer to draw a connection between their work and the impact they have downstream to the customer/consumer.

Consumer values enable managers, senior leaders, and the executive team to make decisions.

Most importantly, they provide focus.

should be by here in about five minutes, can I help you find a spot so you can see it?"

Very simple. Disney cast members are trained to MAKE IT EASY for every guest in the resort.

I hope these examples of KNOW ME, SURPRISE ME, MAKE IT EASY offer further clarity and value as you think about your own organizations' consumer experience strategy. Who knew we could learn so much from a car, a toilet, and a mouse!

Group XP released their report results ranking Tesla number one in customer experience within the automobile industry and 20th overall. The report speaks of Tesla's ability to lead in consumer loyalty and engagement. They are a leader when it comes to consumer impressions, and tied with such brands as Disney and Pampers.

What I Will Do with It ...

I will continue to research and share key learnings from the service industry. As a matter of fact, I will challenge myself to model The Nason Group after some of the most renown service industry leaders. Will my customers get a magic band like Disney? Probably not, but can they expect that I will know them, surprise them, and make it easy? That's a resounding YES!

What You Can Do ...

Where else can you find innovation that inspires you? Be intentional about looking for examples of customer service and write about them, share them, then emulate them as part of your own practice. Seek out experiences to put you into the space where you can just be curious and observant (not judgmental) of the service experience you are in and observe others who may be co-participants in the service line.

CHAPTER 25

Call Yourself an Expert?
Do Yourself a Favor and Don't

"An expert is someone who can tell you exactly how something can't be done"

— **Robert Heinlein** —

Jackie Barretta wrote about the problem of "experts" in a *Fast Company* article, "Why Experts Are the Last People You Want to Include in Creative Brainstorming." Barretta states, "When you help people let go of the idea that so-called experts know it all, you open up the team to fresh ideas, help them forge stronger bonds, and generate better results."

This advice is profound. I was speaking with an organization that was so caught up in making sure they had the right experts in the room in order to reach a consensus in their business model they couldn't make any progress let alone reach agreement. What they didn't seem to understand was that what they were doing had been done again and again. And everyone knows the simple definition of insanity is doing the same thing repeatedly and expecting different results! This organization was going down the same path they have always gone down. They were preoccupied with bringing the same people in the room again and again.

My humble suggestion?

Let the idea of "experts" and "right people in the room" go. Yes, don't invite only experts into your decision-making and brain-storming. Instead, focus on inviting a variety of diverse parties who may bring with them fresh ideas and divergent thinking. Also, if you must have "experts," ask them to leave their name tags, titles, and expertise at the door. Ask them to listen; ask them to open their minds, and invite them to become "sponges."

What? Yes. You heard me, stop calling yourself an expert. Stop expecting others to refer to themselves as self-appointed experts. To pull a retro Susan Powter on you: "Stop the insanity!"

I stopped it. You can, too.

For many years of my professional career, I focused on being an expert. I wanted to be the person who everyone turned to who supposedly "knew it all" in my field. I was once an "expert" in my first career of music. Then I was an "expert" in finance. In the past several years of my career, I have focused on being an "expert" in innovation. However, over the past few months, I've done some thinking on the matter, and I've concluded: I don't want to be an expert in anything.

What I really want to be is a sponge. I want to be the kind of person who *surrounds* himself with others who want to learn, study, and take chances. I want to *absorb* knowledge and information about a variety of subjects and fields, and therefore, enhance and broaden what I already know. I want to continue to be *curious*. I want to

💡 A NOTE FROM STEVE

Consumer-Centered Innovation is a full-contact, inclusive meritocracy — where diverse perspectives are not only welcome but required. Answers are driven from a place of discovery and exploration — everything starts on the table. Expert-driven initiatives often lack the diversity because of "knowing" the answer.

I like Shawn's take on being an expert and from my perspective, there is nothing wrong with being an expert assuming a mindset of learning, and continuous discovery. However, inflexible expertise in a CCI environment lends itself to mediocre results, lack of energy, and buy-in because there is only one correct answer.

I've worked with many experts in a variety of fields. My favorite experts are those people who feel they can always learn more and look at every engagement as an opportunity to fine-tune their expertise and to challenge their knowledge. These people look to increase their expertise not necessarily in their domain but what they know is challenged in the context of a unique organizational culture or business model.

If you are an expert, what's your approach? How much flexibility do you have and how willing are you to stretch? Do you draw others in or shut them down with your expertise? There will always be a place for you; however, that most likely won't be in environments that believe in diversity of thought and use CCI.

acknowledge there is so much more I don't know and so much more I can learn.

Now, I am not advocating throwing away all the knowledge I do have, or recommending others who have spent their individual lifetimes focused on particular areas of study to up and quit, but what I am calling for is a new way of thinking about one's expertise, mainly by advocating that we all drop the "I am an expert" and "I know everything" facades we operate under and that we *adopt a more open-minded approach.*

The idea of approaching anything we do with openness and few preconceptions is scary. Perhaps our greatest obstacle in dealing with higher education and healthcare, in particular, is that everyone in these fields are, by their very virtue, experts in their fields. A WWII history professor is an expert in, you guessed it, WWII. And that's not enough of a specialty by academia's standards. He or she probably wrote a thesis on a particular region, aspect, year, or even person during that period and spent years working to become the preeminent expert in that area. In healthcare — whether one chooses to be a nurse, doctor, technician, or administrator — the varied careers demand that one becomes an expert. (I, for one, want my surgeons to be an "expert" at surgery. I get that). So, what to do? Not be an expert? No. That's not what I am saying.

What I am saying is to change one's mindset whenever approaching something new or different. Instead of calling oneself an expert, be prepared to approach one's work with a new or beginner-like attitude. It's not easy. In fact, it requires a kind of unschooling, which is very difficult in both of those fields, or frankly, in any field. It's counterintuitive. And yet, it's what we must do to embrace new ideas.

Referring to myself as a sponge does not erase my expertise in the fields of music, finance, and innovation. It expands me to grow in those respective fields, as well as affords me the opportunity to explore new ones. It allows me to listen, to ask questions, to be curious, to let my guard down. It allows me to see what is possible, instead of what is NOT.

> What are you an expert in?
> Are you willing to let go of that title?
> How can you become more open to new ideas?
> How might you deal with the experts in your organization?
> How might you help them shift their thinking?
> How might you help move the needle?

I know I am faced with this challenge both in higher education and healthcare. I need help! What are your ideas to help us move the needle?

What I Will Do with It …

I'll keep being the sponge instead of the expert. I will always be curious and not use the expertise I've gained over time to blind me from the potential new learning that I could gain by being curious. I will ensure that customers who entrust me to partner with them on consumer-centric solutions will be included through options that support diversity, so that we can get the greatest amount of perspective as we tackle their biggest challenges.

What You Can Do …

Think about the advantages of working with diversity versus experts as part of your consumer-centric innovation strategy. Experts do have a place in the world, but remember that most people are not experts. They are, in fact, just people who have desires and perspectives that YOU need to understand. A diverse group of individuals will help you to naturally tackle challenges from a variety of perspectives.

Imagine the insanity of designing something specifically for women and not having a single woman on the team — INSANE! More importantly, ensuring that you have a diverse representation of not only women, but those who influence women might be an important first step in this scenario.

CHAPTER 26

Know Me! Surprise Me!
Make It Easy for Me!

Those three simple statements say so much and should be very easy to practice, but it seems like in the world of knowing your consumer and how to best meet their needs it is very difficult. These three principles are nonnegotiable as a leader within any organization I am a part of. They become the way we operate and do business internally and externally.

I was lucky to participate in a roundtable with some dynamic innovation leaders from across several industries. We shared and spoke for several hours on our struggles, challenges, and successes. I had an epiphany during the middle of the session — and it was simple — many of these companies do not know THEIR consumer! These companies were doing wicked cool things, but still had a mentality of BUILD IT AND THEY WILL COME!

Author Sam Milbrath (2016) spotlighted five brands (DeWalt, Lego, DHL, Manchester City FC, and Made.com) that do customer-centric innovation well in their businesses. This leads me to a dynamic leader I worked with in a previous role. This leader was in charge of a consumer experience team in my organization and guided a team of colleagues in developing a strategy to bring to life: Know Me! Surprise Me! Make It Easy for Me! This leader truly understood these principles and how valuable they are to any organization.

A NOTE FROM STEVE

Values are like a tattoo. Once you have them, it is really tough to turn back and "erase" them from the culture or your back! And I suppose that's the point. When the organization, not just senior leadership or the CEO, have a say in values and are focused on the customer and consumer — you begin to change everything about your organization. This cannot be emphasized enough.

Four organizations that had some variation of the values that we use, have each transformed into new organizations. How?

Leadership shifted.

Mindset Shifted.

Culture shifted.

All these shifts enabled the organization to ask bigger, broader questions of themselves and their customers. Knowing your customers and consumers by getting out on the street, participating in co-creation and collaboration with your customers changes lives, strategies, and impact to financials; it becomes a requirement, not an option.

Know that no matter where you are at today, it is never too late to re-discover your customer and consumers.

KNOW ME ...

Cultivate authentic, human connections. Establish new and reinforce existing relationships that provide support, encouragement, inspiration, and accountability for near, as well as, long-term, well-being improvement. Help members engage in their well-being with strategic partners (coaches, those close to them, and those who are "similar strangers.")

Be a trusted guide, partner, and advocate. Listen to members first. Allow them to become vulnerable and reveal their true fears, needs, and desires. Be non-judgmental. Help them focus and choose realistic, personalized goals. Empower them to achieve real and positive change in their well-being. Be there to help them be their best self.

Account for the whole person and the context of their daily life. Have empathy for your members. Solve their problems. Be respectful of their time, desire, and ability. Engage them in the ways they choose. Meet them where they are. Help them integrate the things they need to do for their well-being into the lives they already lead.

SURPRISE ME ...

Harness knowledge to provide novel, useful, and actionable insights. Use what we learn about each individual to offer personal and targeted insights, feedback, content, and next steps. Remember what we've learned about the member.

Give them realistic, personalized action plans that align with THEIR definition of what well-being looks like. Provide insights and connections that the consumer might not discover on their own.

MAKE IT EASY ...

Deliver a consistently frictionless experience. Understand how real users interact. Make every interaction effective and simple. Provide seamless integration regardless of channel (digital, on-site, phone, paper.) Ensure each piece of the experience feels like part of a whole. Use what we've learned from our successes and failures to continuously improve the experience for our members.

Another, "aha" moment I experienced is that these companies practiced innovation, but not Customer-Centric Innovation. In today's times, we as leaders, must not separate the two. They must work hand-in-hand and be the center of how an organization functions operationally. In the blog post, "Is the Customer Always Right?" by Jennifer Lee of Deloitte, she talks about the future of Consumer-Driven Innovation. She simply states that to make Customer-Centric Innovation successful you must understand how you will work with customers — as well as why!

What I Will Do with It ...

I am going to be relentless in sharing these consumer principles - I may even get a tattoo of the three of them to show true commitment! Seriously, these principles are the foundation of how I live my life, how I lead, and I how I engage and work with my customers and partners.

More needs to be done to articulate the value of using these principles in my everyday work, and through each interaction I have throughout the day. In the very near future, I plan to share more about how to lead using a more in-depth application of these principles.

What You Can Do ...

Ask yourself the following about your current consumers and those that you either lead, support, or follow:

1. How well do I know them?

2. How can I surprise them so they have that "aha" moment?

3. How can I make it easy for them to consume our product or service, or make it easy for my leader to lead me or those who report to me — to make it easy to become leaders and follow me?

CHAPTER 27

Surprise, Surprise! – The Ability to SURPRISE Your Consumer!

Many have heard me say, that it only takes three principles to build a consumer experience model. Those three principles are simple: Know Me, Surprise Me, and Make It Easy! That is where the hard part comes in, keeping it simple!

> *"Simple can be harder than complex: You have to work hard to get your thinking clean to make it simple. But it's worth it in the end because once you get there, you can move mountains."*
>
> **— Steve Jobs —**

The story goes something like this: There once was a family visiting Walt Disney World. It was a beautiful fall morning, and the family had just finished breakfast at Disney's Animal Kingdom. They were waiting to use their next fast pass, so they decided to do some window shopping. At one of the confectionery shops, they came across an amazing display of caramel apples that looked like different animals. A Disney cast member greeted the family with a simple, "Hello!" As the family was standing there admiring the creative work, the daughter looked up to her father and asked if she could have one (now remember, they had just finished breakfast.) The father told his daughter, "Honey, not now! We just finished eating."

The family went to leave the store to make their way to the ride when the father felt a slight tap on his shoulder. He turned around, and it was that cast member. The cast member politely asked if she could present a small gift to his daughter. The father said, "YES!" What the father did not know is that the cast member had been listening so well, she'd heard the girl ask specifically for the elephant caramel apple. And, there it was, in a lovely box ready to give to her. The little girl was so happy and asked her father if she could keep it. Well, of course, the father had to say, "Yes!"

This story is about my family and my daughter. Now, some people might have been upset over the interaction, but to be frank, I was totally SURPRISED! That cast member knew we could afford to buy that apple, but they wanted to do something unforgettable and incredibly powerful for my daughter and me.

What I Learned ...

That experience happened months ago — and yet, it is still fresh in my mind. It was so simple for that cast member to provide an unforgettable experience. She lived out the principles of Know Me, Surprise Me, Make it Easy to a tee. She took the time to listen.

Here is my learning: listen, listen, listen! The cast member got to KNOW my family and ME in a short period by listening to our conversation. She saw an opportunity to SURPRISE ME by getting to my daughter's heart, and in doing so, created a magical experience for me as well. Finally, she MADE IT EASY with a single five-dollar apple. For the rest of that day, my daughter could talk of nothing else but the experience of receiving that little elephant.

"Speak in such a way that others love to listen to you. Listen in such a way that others love to speak to you!"

What We Can Do ...

Listening is a simple concept, but again, sometimes it is also the most complicated thing to do. I will LISTEN to those around me. Whether it is my wife, my children, a co-worker, or our consumer.

♀ A NOTE FROM STEVE

Shawn is a great storyteller and I am a great story collector. I love Shawn's call to action to basically get out and talk to people. It is so simple yet something many of us choose not to do.

Oftentimes, regardless of location, I observe and listen to what is going on around me. In many cases, asking one or two simple questions about an experience encourages people to speak at length. They are really giving us a gift — even if it isn't about the industry or situation that is directly applicable. The more stories we collect, the greater the empathy leading to important insights.

We gain the most by listening. Through building empathy and gathering insights, we are able to better Know, Surprise, and Make It Easy for our customers and consumers.

We all have a listen-learning story, and it deserves to be heard. As a matter of fact, consumers expect and demand it today. Mason Thelon in his article from "Mad Men' to 'Math Men': Listen to Your Customers Not Your Gut" discusses three main concepts around personalization, silos, and technology. The customer is telling us what they want; we just have to LISTEN!

Take 30 minutes this week. Hit the streets! Listen to those around you. Get to know your consumer or customer. They will tell you what they want and need. It is our job to take it to the next level.

Remember this: KNOW ME, SURPRISE ME, and MAKE IT EASY!

Final Thoughts

Saying YES! to the Power of Innovation really involves three key elements: Mindset, Leadership, and defining your consumer principles or values.

First, focus on shifting your mindset and being open to speaking with consumers to inform your product or service. It is not uncommon for us to bring in consumers to collaborate and co-create on potential solutions — going well beyond the focus group.

Secondly, leadership is incredibly important in shifting the organization to a consumer-centered innovation focus. Without leadership, it is a long and painful road. Some of our innovation colleagues have been suffering through the scenario of trying to set up innovation within organizations without leadership being at the center of the transformation and helping navigate the storm of cultural resistance.

Lastly, decide on your consumer principles or values. Use these principles (or feel free to steal the ones we ascribe to) in order to frame everything you do to better know your consumer, surprise them with that "ache" or moment of delight, and make it easy for them to use your product or service.

We hope that this primer on The Power of YES! in Innovation has opened up your mind and heart to consumer-centered innovation.

We know from our perspective that pulling together the major elements of the book has reconfirmed our passion to being consumer champions and enabling our partners to put the consumer at the center of everything they do.

Several gentle reminders as you impart on your journey.

It's Not About Me! It's about those around us. Jack Welch reminded all of us of this in his quote, *"The day you become a leader, your job is to take people who are already great and make them unbelievable."*

Design Leads Strategy. This is not always easy, but it is right.

Simplify, Simplify, Simplify. Steve Jobs stated, *"Simple can be harder than complex: You have to work hard to get your thinking clean to make it simple. But it's worth it in the end because once you get there, you can move mountains."*

Conquer Your Fears! You can do anything you put your mind to — even if you do not believe you can! As a leader, father, husband, friend, or just as a person, I must remember these three things: be honest with myself, make the behavior my own, and take the plunge.

Know Me! Surprise Me! Make It Easy! In the spirit of simplicity, quit making everything so difficult for consumers. Live by these three principles, and you will hit it out of the park.

Richard Branson stated, *"If someone offers you an amazing opportunity and you are not sure you can do it, say yes. Then learn how to do it later."*

And if you need a partner in saying YES!, we will be here for you.

A NOTE FROM STEVE

In order to transform the organization into one leveraging CCI, leadership is absolutely key in demonstrating that the customer is the most important aspect of the business. Everyone watches leaders for their queues.

Leadership is key in developing the mindset required to transform an organization. Move from a focus on products and services only, to one that delivers value to the customer through the products and services they offer by welcoming the insights that customers and consumers can provide.

Culture is built upon the actions of leaders and colleagues. Cultures that leverage CCI are unique. The focus CCI provides on the customer and consumer drives behavior, decision-making, investments and even profitability. It is a profound shift and you will make mistakes along the way. The good news is that with the focus on the customer and consumer, you will always find your way back quickly.

References

Malofsky, Adam. Innovation is a lifestyle, not a bunch of metrics! [Web log comment]. Retrieved from *https://www.linkedin.com/pulse/20140528231717-3412513-innovation-is-a-lifestyle-not-a-bunch-of-metrics*

Milbrith, Sam. (2016, August 5). Co-creation: Five examples of brands driving customer-driven innovation. [Web log comment]. Retrieved from *https://www.visioncritical.com/5-examples-how-brands-are-using-co-creation/*

Song, Jean. (2015, February 4). XPrize CEO talks boldness, breakthroughs. CBS News. Retrieved from *http://www.cbsnews.com/news/xprize-ceo-peter-diamandis-on-how-to-create-impact-new-book-bold/*

About the Authors

Shawn Nason

"Innovation Isn't Work, Innovation is a Lifestyle!" Those words accurately describe the roles he has had in his eclectic career; however, it does not describe the amazing journey he has been on and how he got to where he is today.

That journey to where he is today and what he is passionate about is personal. He can't help it, and he's comfortable challenging the system that could have better helped him take care of both of his parents. As a result of these experiences, he chose to relentlessly pursue innovations in how healthcare can flip the model to put the consumer at the center of its approach. He describes himself as the Chief Consumer Champion!

Fast forward to today. Shawn has been blessed to start The Nason Group, where their focus is to help their *partners* meet their *consumers* where they are, to better inform how those partners approach current and future products and services. While he has deep passion for healthcare, the tools Shawn and his colleagues employ to impact healthcare are universal and accessible in the context of any organization that wants to join them on the journey toward *consumer-centered innovation.*

Shawn has learned through his career that deeply listening to the consumer is a key tenet of successful organizations and a bold move for leaders to undertake. His challenge to both small and large organizations is to evaluate deeply your commitment to the consumer. If you aren't where you feel you need to be, go find someone (it doesn't have to be The Nason Group) to help you put the consumer at the center of the products and services you offer.

In his free time, Shawn loves to travel, shop, play, and aggravate his amazing family: Carla, Kayla, and Kolby. Shawn also enjoys playing a little bit of poker when he can, or hitting the sticks.

Contact Shawn at *shawn@nasongroup.co.*

Steve Junion

First in his family to graduate college, Steve landed a job shortly after college as a Computing Technology Network Systems Engineer with no experience in the Information Technology industry. His success in this role and his background in training from the military and college led him to becoming a senior technical instructor of enterprise operating systems and architecture solutions. During this time, Steve found himself innovating  with early web-based virtual classroom technology, including voice-over-internet protocol (VOIP) as well as content distribution networks. Through trial and error, Steve learned the value of what it takes to create a successful online classroom experience through building communities. Since these early days, his career has been eclectic at best, and sporadic at worse. Steve, a self-proclaimed expert of the Gen X generation, consistently refers to his experiences related to work as "career skydiving."

During the past five years, Steve has taken his expertise in designing learning experiences to the consumer-centered innovation design space. A natural transition from developing learning and leadership development experiences, Steve quickly became comfortable with the tools and processes in this space. He's found himself creating a number of consumer-focused experiences in business for a Fortune 100 health and wellbeing organization, while also leading other teams in pursuit of putting the consumer at the center of their solutions.

As Steve seeks to reinvent himself and build on his past experiences, he is relentlessly focusing on creating a new vision for himself. This vision includes being recognized internationally as a designer of experiences that help executives, leaders, and teams solve complex, large-scale international problems to positively impact the business, consumers, and the communities they serve.

In his free time, Steve spends time with Cheryl, his wife, and three kids — Seth, MJ, and Drew — at various sporting events or telling mostly true stories about his life. He also loves talking about personal finance, and playing episodes of the Dave Ramsey show to irritate Shawn.

Contact Steve at *sdjunion@gmail.com.*

Made in the USA
Middletown, DE
05 November 2019